W9-AVM-093

ANIMAL BEHAVIOR

ANIMAL BEHAVIOR

General Editor: Tim Halliday

University of Oklahoma Press : Norman

Published by the University of Oklahoma Press,
Norman, Publishing Division of the University

Produced by
Weldon Russell Pty Ltd
107 Union Street, North Sydney,
NSW 2060, Australia
A member of the Weldon International
Group of Companies

Library of Congress Cataloging-in-Publication Data
Animal behavior / general editor, Tim Halliday
p. cm.
Includes index
ISBN 0–8061–2647–7
1. Animal behavior. I. Halliday, Tim, 1945–
QL751.A6493 1994 93–42912
591.51—dc20 CIP

Publishing Manager: Susan Hurley
Project Co-ordinator: Kayte Nunn
Editor: Alison Pressley
Picture Researcher: Anne Nicol
Designer: Rowena Sheppard
Macintosh Layout Artist: Stuart McVicar
Illustrators: Barbara Rodanska and Jan Smith
Captions: Carson Creagh
Indexer: Michael Wyatt
Production: Dianne Leddy

Produced by Mandarin Offset, Hong Kong
Printed and bound in China

A KEVIN WELDON PRODUCTION

Photographs: endpapers: bullfrog; page 3: king penguins; page 5: mountain gorilla; page 6: tiger; page 7, top left: flamingos; page 7, top right: Japanese macaques; page 7, bottom left: Masai giraffe; page 7, bottom right: Mauritius day gecko; page 8, left: orang-utan; page 8, bottom: European bee-eaters; page 9, top: arctic hares; page 9, right: Florida panther; page 9, bottom: strawberry poisondart frogs.

CONTENTS

INTRODUCTION

Professor Tim Halliday

Animals live and move about within a prescribed area during the course of their lives. They share their habitats with other animals, of the same and of different species, and they have particular kinds of relationships with those other animals. They may compete with individuals of the same and of different species for space and food. One species may be a predator, another its prey. At some time in their life, most animals mate and, in doing so, establish a relationship with another member of their species. This book is about the many kinds of interactions that occur between animals, their physical habitat and their biological world.

The modern science of animal behavior, called ethology, grew out of natural history studies in which naturalists simply described the habits of living animals, often in great detail. This observational and descriptive approach was made more rigorous and was set in a scientific framework in the 1950s by the two pioneers of ethology, Niko Tinbergen and Konrad Lorenz. Lorenz, working in Germany, made two major contributions to the developing science. First, he showed how early experience of their parents influences the social behavior of birds such as ducks and geese. Most notably, he described how geese, hand-reared by him, followed him around as goslings and, as adults, tried to mate with him. Second, his work on the courtship rituals of ducks revealed how each species has a repertoire

of behavior patterns that is as characteristic of that species as its plumage or the sound it makes. From this, he argued that the behavior of a species has evolved by natural selection and is adapted to the particular habitat and way of life of that species.

Niko Tinbergen, working in Holland and later in Britain, shared Lorenz's interests in the development of behavior during an animal's life and in its evolutionary history. He is best known, however, for his work on what causes behavior. What are the immediate conditions, or stimuli, that trigger a particular pattern of behavior? He showed, for example, that male sticklebacks are stimulated to attack other males by their red color, but to court females by their swollen, silvery belly. One of Tinbergen's important contributions was to show how observations of behavior can be organized and made more systematic by posing a series of simple and specific questions, such as "What causes behavior to happen?", "How does behavior develop over time?" and "What is the survival value of a particular pattern of behavior?"

Lorenz, Tinbergen, and other early ethologists used simple tools to observe, record, and describe the behavior of animals. They needed little more than a hide, a pair of binoculars, and a notebook. Today, technology is widely used to study animal behavior. Migrating birds are tracked by radar, diving whales and seals carry depth recorders, and whether or not birds mate with individuals other than their partner can be determined by DNA fingerprinting. Useful as such technical advances are, the basics of studying animal behavior remain the same; before detailed questions can be asked about animal behavior, the behavior itself must be carefully and meticulously described. What follows in this book is based on such descriptions.

From Birth to Maturity

COURTING RITUALS

Dr. Charlotte A. Hosie

The New Guinea birds of paradise show off their flashy feathers; the tiny manakins of South America execute tumbling acrobatics; European blackbirds sing rich, complex melodies; the silk moth produces a sexy scent. These animals are all performing the rituals of courtship, a dazzling array of displays encompassing sight, sound, touch, and smell.

But such displays may take a great deal of effort and require lots of energy. At the same time, by advertising their presence so boldly, animals risk attracting the unwelcome attention of a passing predator.

So why do they go to so much trouble? Why not just mate with any member of the opposite sex that happens to pass by? Some animals do, and only a very perfunctory courtship takes place. However, most animals use more complex courting rituals, shaped by such factors as their environment, and whether or not they live in social groups. Some may have to fight vicious battles for mates, or spend hours displaying to attract them from afar. Animals have solved the problems involved in finding a mate with an endless variety of courtship tactics.

Courtship rituals may serve many purposes: to bring the sexes together; to increase sexual receptivity; to enable females to assess males; to allow males to determine a female's readiness to mate; and to coordinate the act of mating itself.

Finding a mate

For some animals, merely establishing contact with a potential partner presents a major challenge. A male great argus pheasant, living a solitary existence in dense tropical forest in Malaysia, has first to attract females to him before considering anything more fancy by way of a display. He does this by repeating a distinctive call that travels great distances through the thick forest vegetation. Females can then

Above: Ritual fighting is used by species such as impalas to establish the dominance of a particular male and so gain the favors of a harem of females. Many of these fighting contests follow highly elaborate rules.
Left: Male peacocks display together and the female mates with the one that exhibits the most complex form of color pattern.

△ *The spectacular plumage of the magnificent riflebird stands out in the forests of New Guinea and northeast Australia. The male frequently displays his bright, iridescent plumage to his duller, generally brown partner from particular bare branches within their shared territory, where he is shown off to best advantage.*

make their way to the source of the calls and meet up with the male. Once they are in visual contact, the male's elaborate plumes—similar to those of the more familiar peacock—come into their own as he performs ritualized dances for the female.

Not far from where the argus pheasant dances, the males of a large toad species space out along the rainforest river banks to call. Every night, as dusk settles, the toads move into their individual sites and begin calling. The call consists of a series of very loud resonant "bops," which increase in intensity to a climax of four or five waves of cascading notes, ringing up and down the river. Each male repeats these over and over until dawn, when he ceases this exhausting effort to attract females.

Groups bring choice—and fights

Not all animals have to go to such lengths in their courtship simply to attract a potential mate. Living in social groups means that meeting the opposite sex is not difficult, but it may bring other problems. It is often the case that all the females in a group are sexually receptive together. All the female ring-tailed lemurs of Madagascar, for instance, come into estrus over two weeks in April, each one being receptive for less than a single day. The courting rituals of this species consist of fighting between males rather than decorative displays directed toward the females. A male will cover his strikingly banded tail with his own scent, then point it forward over his head to fend off rivals. At the peak of the mating period, fending-off behavior escalates to vicious, bloody battles for the females.

In many group-living species, courtship involves the male assessing whether females are ready to mate. In the class of mammals called ungulates, which includes gazelles and bison, the male sniffs the female's urine and genitals by curling his upper lip in a distinctive way (called the "flehmen" test). This tells him about her hormonal state and whether she is sexually receptive. Some gazelles, such as the African gerenuk, perform slightly more sophisticated rituals involving head movements, followed by the male tapping on the female's hindlegs with his forelegs before curling his lip in the flehmen gesture.

Increasing sexual receptivity

Males of many species of deer perform ritualized courtship displays, usually involving well-developed antlers. These are used to maintain or contest access to a group of females. However, in red deer the powerful roaring of the stags has another function: it helps to bring the females into a sexually receptive condition. In fact, the courtship displays of many animals serve multiple functions. They may be crucial for increasing the sexual receptivity of one or both sexes, as well as coordinating the physical act of mating.

The male of the North American red-spotted newt captures the female, then clasps her firmly to him (a behavior pattern called "amplexus"), and holds her in this position for up to three hours. During this time he rubs the scent glands sited on his cheek across the female's snout, and beats his tail to create a water current above her head. By the time he releases her from amplexus, she is sexually receptive and correctly positioned to follow him through the next stage of courtship, when she can become inseminated.

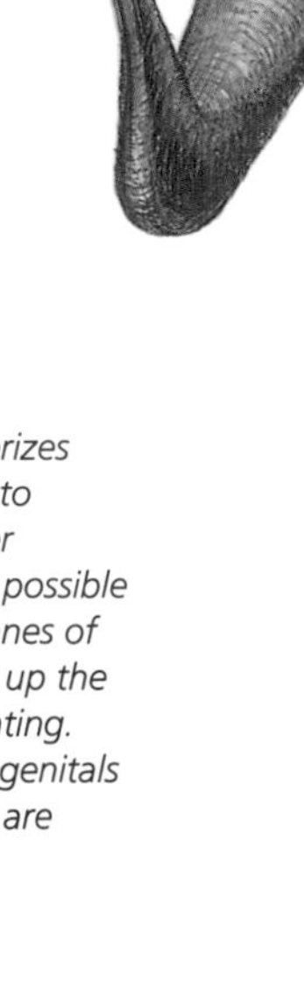

▷ *The curled lip that characterizes the flehmen gesture common to sheep, bison, horses, and other ungulates exposes as much as possible of the odor-detecting membranes of the mouth and nostrils to pick up the scent of a female ready for mating. Male animals sniff at females' genitals and urine to determine if they are sexually receptive.*

△ *Some animals increase the sexual receptivity of their mates by elaborate courtship displays. A male European crested newt beats his tail rhythmically to create a current that carries his odor from his cloaca to her snout. If this stimulation makes her receptive, she approaches him and he leads her over his sperm, contained in a spermataphore.*

◁ *Ring-tailed lemurs have evolved a means of settling rivalries without immediately resorting to violence. Males coat their bushy tails with their own scent, then carry their distinctively banded tails over their heads to fend off rivals. At the peak of the one-day mating period, however, competition becomes so fierce that bloody battles erupt between competing males.*

△ *The male Victoria riflebird of Australia displays on a sunlit tree stump or in the crown of a tree. Raising his wings until the tips meet over his head, he sways and pivots his body, his green-tipped body plumes fanned out. He moves his head rhythmically from side to side, uttering a rasping call to attract females.*

Breathtaking displays

In some 90 percent of bird species, a male and female will pair off for the whole of a breeding season, if not for life. Both sexes usually help to feed and care for the young. Among the remaining ten percent of bird species, males and females do not form pairs. After a very brief copulation, the male contributes nothing to bringing up the young birds. Although they constitute a very small proportion of all birds, these non-monogamous species have received a vast amount of attention and study by many people interested in animal behavior. This is primarily because they have the most dramatic, extravagant, and breathtaking courting rituals of all.

A fine example of the extent to which some non-monogamous male birds will develop their feathers in order to court females is the shimmering train of the peacock. This is fanned out to show off iridescent green and bronze eye spots, and shaken so that the feathers rattle.

Many of the birds of paradise of New Guinea and Australia have raised feather elaboration to an art form. The common names of some of them reflect the magnificence of their plumage: king bird of paradise, ribbon-tailed, twelve-wired, and King of Saxony. Another species, Lawes' parotia, at first appears quite plain—all black with a green breast shield—but he manipulates his feathers dramatically when a female is present at his display court. He flares his flank feathers into a skirt, stretches his neck, and hops slowly from one foot to the other. Then he shakes his breast shield and his head from side to side, until the long black-tipped feathers on his forehead become a blur.

The Victoria riflebird also appears rather drab until he suddenly stretches and spreads his wing feathers with a dramatic flourish, so that they resemble a sweeping black cloak. At the same time, he fluffs up an iridescent shield which spreads across his breast.

HIDE AND SEEK

Male tragopan pheasants, found in Asia, boast colorful plumage while the female has a much plainer, more subdued set of feathers, as with most non-monogamous birds. Male tragopans also have fleshy blue horns on the head, which can be erected as part of the display, and intriguing colorful throat lappets which they inflate. They have two kinds of display, lateral and frontal. The lappet and horns are used in the frontal courtship display.

A male Temminck's tragopan starts by hiding behind a rock and peering over at the female. He then twitches his head and gradually begins to expose his throat lappet and horns to the female. He spreads his tail and begins to beat his wings, which makes the horns vibrate. After a few seconds he utters repeated clicking calls in synchrony with the wingbeats. At the climax of the display the male hisses, rises up, and spreads his wings downward, inflating the lappet to its fullest. He may then run over the top of the rock and approach the female to copulate.

△ *Satyr tragopan.*
◁ *Temminck's tragopan.*

Bowerbirds and Their Bowers

A family of birds closely related to the birds of paradise is distinctive not because its members have decorative feathers, but for the elaborate constructions they build as part of their courtship rituals. These are the bowerbirds of New Guinea and North Australia. Different species show varying levels of architectural ability, but all have a painstaking approach to their work.

The toothed bowerbird is also known as the stagemaker. He clears an area of forest floor up to 8 feet (2.5 m) across, carefully removing all debris. He cuts leaves from particular trees using his toothed bill and lays them on the "stage," pale side uppermost, so they are obvious in the dim light of the forest. Withered leaves are replaced each day with fresh ones. When the stage is set, the male sits above it and sings. If a female appears, he goes down to the stage and performs a crouched display, flicking his wings and tail.

Slightly more complex are the avenue bowers cleared by, among others, Archbold's bowerbird. They are decorated with piles of snail shells, beetles' wings, berries, and molted bird of paradise feathers.

Birds of the third group of bower builders construct two parallel walls of twigs and heap their decorations at each end. White pebbles, bones, and shells are the choice of the spotted bowerbird, while Lauterbach's bowerbird favors gray and red objects. The satin bowerbird has a preference for blue objects—including, where human debris is available, blue bottle tops and pieces of blue plastic. He also goes a step farther in his decorations and pulps blue berries to paint the inside of the bower's walls.

The prize for structural complexity of bowers must go to the "maypole builders"; these birds use saplings as a central support for towers of twigs. MacGregor's bowerbird constructs a single maypole, while the golden bowerbird builds a pair of towers and links them with decorated bridges. But the gardener bowerbird outshines all with his "hut" of twigs 3 feet (1 m) high and 6 feet (2 m) across. The entrance has a garden of moss and piles of brightly colored flowers and fruit.

△ There are 18 species of bowerbird. The males of the species, such as this gold and black regent bowerbird, are strikingly colored.

◁ The male satin bowerbird collects bright blue objects to adorn the stage around the bower. He then positions himself on the display area and dances with a colored object to attract the female.

△ *Not only does the male lyrebird display his magnificent tail plumes to attract females, but he also imitates, with uncanny accuracy, the calls of birds and mammals—even the sounds of humans and their domestic animals —to demonstrate the size and complexity of his territory; in effect, advertising that he controls a food supply that is more than sufficient to support a 'family.'*

Choosy females

It is easy to see why birds such as the bowerbirds, birds of paradise, and tragopans have attracted so much human attention. In 1874, long before courtship behavior in animals was studied in any systematic way, Charles Darwin noted the incredible sexual dimorphism (differences in physical appearance) these birds exhibit. The females of the species are invariably a brownish color, while the males usually show some kind of plumage exhibitionism. Darwin felt that the cause "seems to lie in the males having stronger passions than the females." It is perhaps doubtful whether males do indeed have stronger passions, but it is more clear that the two sexes approach courtship from rather different perspectives.

It is generally recognized that males produce lots of sperm and can potentially inseminate large numbers of females. In contrast, females produce far fewer eggs than a male does sperm, and often bear the greater burden of parental duty. As she produces relatively few eggs in her lifetime, a female has proportionately more invested in each of these than the male does in each of his millions of sperm. When this is the case, male animals tend to try and mate with as many females as possible to maximize their lifetime's reproductive output. Females, because they invest so much in each egg, are rather more selective about their mates. It could be said that males go for quantity while females are more swayed by quality.

But if the male provides the female with nothing except sperm, how can she determine the quality she seeks in males? This is where elaborate courtship displays and ornate feathers come in. It is known that females do appear to mate with the more ornate males; peahens, for example, prefer peacocks with a larger number of eye spots on their trains. The males of many of these highly decorated bird species display quite close to each other or cluster on arenas called "leks" (the Swedish word for playground). Females assess individual males before mating with one in particular.

Different theories abound as to why females might choose the more elaborate males. Possessing flashy plumage may be costly to the male in terms of the energy required to grow and maintain it and of the risk of attracting predators. So it may be that the better developed his fancy feathers, the more accomplished a male is at the art of survival. The chances are that the offspring of these males will also have better survival qualities.

▷ *Courtship feeding, the ritual exchange of food during mating or to reinforce the bond between a mated pair, occurs in many groups of animals; indeed, some biologists believe it is the origin of human kissing. A male dance-fly presents his mate with a banquet in the form of a mosquito, which she consumes while copulation takes place.*

You are what you eat

It is evident that courtship can be very important in enabling a female to assess potential partners and choose a suitable mate. Male guppies living in the rivers of Trinidad show spots of different colors while courting the females. The females tend to prefer to mate with those males that show more orange coloration. This may be a reliable indication of his ability to find appropriate food, since the orange color is synthesized from carotenoids which can only be obtained from the diet, and which are also scarce and so difficult to find. Other colors are more easily manufactured from components already present in the male's body.

Females of the North American red-backed salamander make even more direct assessments of males' feeding habits. They sample a male's feces by "nose-tapping": pressing the snout repeatedly into the dropping. These salamanders prefer to eat juicy thin-skinned termites, which are a richer food source than the hard-skinned ants they may also take. Females can discern the contents of males' diets by nose-tapping their droppings, preferring those that have been feeding on termites.

Gifts of food

Many insects present the female with a courtship gift of food. Most bushcrickets manufacture a spermatophore consisting of a large edible part and a smaller section full of sperm. Females only accept the larger spermatophores, and eat the food part while the sperm are transferred to her body. The male hangingfly captures flies to present to the female. After catching a suitable gift, he performs a short flight and releases a scent attractive to females. When a female approaches he proffers the gift. She accepts only larger flies, and only when she has begun to eat can the male mate with her.

The courtship rituals animals perform may reflect the criteria upon which females base their choice, which can depend largely upon how much the male is involved in caring for the offspring. Common terns and sandwich terns, for instance, pair monogamously after a long courtship period which includes the male catching and presenting small fish to the female. This ability to bring food to the female in courtship reflects how well he will be able to feed the chicks later, so the female can assess the parental skills of potential mates during the courtship stage.

△ *In much the same way as male birds sing to attract females, or male crickets and grasshoppers stridulate, male hissing cockroaches of Madagascar stimulate females during courtship by expelling air from tiny holes on their abdomens.*

Accomplished musicians

Often, the kinds of stimuli that can be employed during courtship depend on the physical constraints imposed by the environment in which the animals live. If, like the argus pheasant in dense tropical forest, individuals cannot see each other, acoustic or olfactory signals may be the only way of communicating.

Calling and song in birds are obvious examples of strongly acoustic courtship displays, but some amphibians and insects are also accomplished musicians. In many frog species, calling is critical in attracting a mate. Indeed, the auditory systems of females have evolved so that they are only responsive to the sound frequency of the calls of males of the same species.

Crickets signal by rubbing their legs against special structures to produce "chirps." The male mole cricket goes a step further. He digs and calls from a large two-chambered burrow to amplify his courtship song. Male hissing cockroaches of Madagascar expel air from tiny holes in their abdomens. This hissing provides vital acoustic stimulation for the female during courtship.

MATING AND BIRTH

Professor Tim Halliday

There is enormous diversity among animals in the form of the mating act, in how long a single mating act lasts, and in how often individuals mate. This diversity arises because there is much more to mating than simply bringing eggs and sperm together. Because eggs are very much larger than sperm, females produce them in much smaller numbers than males produce sperm. As a result, the reproductive success of a female is determined by how many eggs she can produce, and that of a male is determined by the number of females he mates with. There is therefore intrinsic competition among males for sexual access to females, and females are expected to be selective about which males they mate with. Much of the complexity and diversity of mating behavior arises because males must compete with other males and because females are choosy.

The benefits of internal fertilization

For most frogs and many fishes, mating and birth occur at the same moment: eggs and sperm are released simultaneously and they meet outside the parents' bodies. This is called external fertilization, in contrast to internal fertilization, which occurs inside the body of one of the parents, usually the female. Internal fertilization involves a separation in time between mating and birth, the eggs undergoing part of their early development inside the parent's body, and it represents an evolutionary advance on external fertilization.

Internal fertilization is advantageous in a number of ways. It enables mating and birth to be separated in time so that females can give birth at an optimal moment, when a male may not be available. This is important for many spiders, in which encounters

Above: Male praying mantids are occasionally attacked by the female during mating. The female begins by eating his head, then his thorax, but because the nervous system in his abdomen remains intact, sperm continues to be transferred.
Left: The red-eyed leaf frog of Central America lays its eggs on the leaves of trees overhanging streams: the eggs hatch into tadpoles, which drop into the water below.

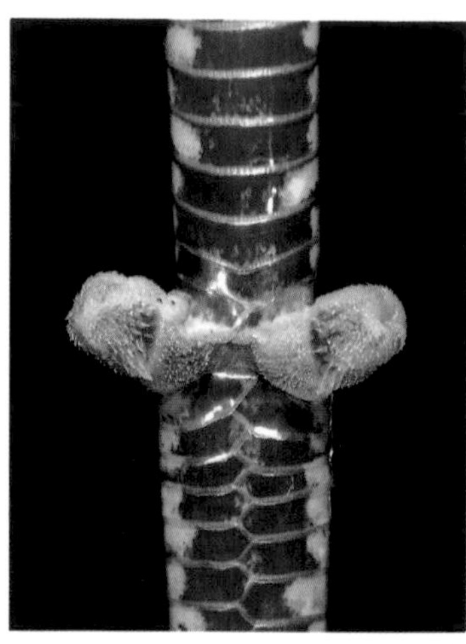

△ *Male snakes and lizards have paired reproductive organs called hemipenes. The male inserts one or other hemipenis into the female's cloaca, where its numerous spines hold it in place.*

between males and females are rare events and may not occur at times or in places that are suitable for giving birth. In European newts, females carefully wrap each fertilized egg in a leaf, a device for protecting the eggs that would not be possible if the male had to be present at the moment of birth. Internal fertilization also means that the young begin their development in the safe environment provided by their mother's body cavity, where they can be nourished directly, as in mammals.

The main disadvantage of internal fertilization is that it limits a female's fecundity (the number of young she can produce) to the number that can be contained within the confines of her body and can then grow to the size needed for birth. Animals with external fertilization typically produce many more eggs at each mating than their counterparts with internal fertilization.

Timing is everything

During mating in which fertilization is external, the male must release his sperm at the same moment as the female releases her eggs. If sperm are released too early, they are likely to be dispersed before meeting the eggs; if they are released too late, the brief period when the eggs can be penetrated by sperm may have passed. Good timing is also important when there is competition for females. In many frogs and fishes, receptive females are in short supply and mating pairs attract males without mates. These males attempt to "sneak" matings by releasing their sperm when the eggs are released, so that a mating male who releases his sperm too late will have reduced reproductive success.

Reproductive organs

A wide variety of animals, including many insects, scorpions, and salamanders, have internal fertilization, but the male has no penis. In spiders, males have special mating organs called pedipalps. During mating, the male extrudes a drop of sperm onto the ground or onto his web. He then sucks up some of the sperm in one of his pedipalps and transfers them to the female's genital opening.

In some species of insects, scorpions, and salamanders, the male has no organ for transferring sperm. Instead, the sperm are contained in a special receptacle, called a spermatophore, that is passed from male to female during mating. The spermatophores of salamanders consist of a sac of sperm placed on top of a gelatinous base. During mating, the female is persuaded to walk over the spermatophore by the male, so that the sperm cap can be removed from its base by her cloaca. In many insects the spermatophore also consists of two parts, one filled with sperm, the other with nutrients that are either eaten by the female or taken up by her genital tract during the mating act.

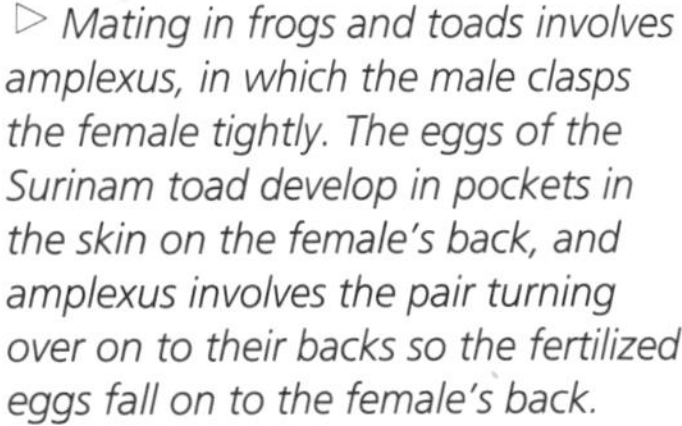

▷ *Mating in frogs and toads involves amplexus, in which the male clasps the female tightly. The eggs of the Surinam toad develop in pockets in the skin on the female's back, and amplexus involves the pair turning over on to their backs so the fertilized eggs fall on to the female's back.*

Despite the fact that birds have internal fertilization, male birds have no penis, but achieve sperm transfer by pressing their genital opening against that of the female. Ducks and geese have a spiral organ, which is not a true penis, that has a groove along its length along which the sperm pass.

In mammals, the penis is an erectile organ that becomes rigid during mating through the hydraulic pressure of blood pumped into it. In some species, such as badgers, whales, and most primates, the penis gains additional support in the form of a penis bone, called the bacculum. In some animals, such as cats, the penis is equipped with hooks or spines that keep it in place during mating.

Snakes and lizards have paired organs called hemipenes. Each hemipenis is a sac which, during mating, is turned inside out like the finger of a glove. In many species there are a number of ridges and spines on the inside of the sac, which thus project outwards during mating and hold the hemipenis in place inside the female's cloaca. The male uses only one of his hemipenes at a time, depending on which side of him the female happens to be, and there is a tendency for left and right hemipenes to be used alternately. The spines on the hemipenes, like those on the penis of cats and many other mammals, serve to hold the male's organ in place; they probably also fulfill the important function of stimulating the female and making her more receptive.

The intrinsically competitive nature of mating is expressed in some dragonflies and millipedes by the possession of a complex penis that serves a dual function. Special appendages on the penis scrape or suck from the female's genital tract any sperm left there by previous matings. Only when the male has removed the sperm of his rivals does a male insert his own sperm.

Mating duration

In birds and many other animals, mating is an extremely brief affair, completed in a few seconds. In several species, however, mating lasts several hours or days. Some salamanders and newts, for example, remain clasped together in a posture called amplexus for several days. Prolonged amplexus may serve one or more of several functions. On most occasions when a male newt meets a female she is not yet sexually receptive, and amplexus provides the male with the opportunity he needs to stimulate her until she becomes ready to mate. In the Californian newt, the male maintains amplexus not only before but also after mating, guarding the female until she becomes unreceptive again, so that she will not subsequently be mated by another male. In many frogs and toads a prolonged amplexus prior to mating, perhaps lasting several days, enables a male to defend a female against the attentions of other males until she is ready to lay her eggs.

The risks of mating

Mating may involve a number of risks. A pair of animals locked in amplexus may be relatively immobile and provide a conspicuous target for potential predators. Male American toads are markedly less ready to engage in amplexus with females at ponds where predatory ravens are present.

Because mating involves physical contact, it provides an opportunity for parasites and sexually transmitted diseases to infect new individuals. This may explain why, in many species, mating is a rare and brief event, though very little is known about the impact of venereal diseases in animals.

In many spiders, the male is very much smaller than the female and so runs the risk of being mistaken by her for a prey item. Some male spiders signal to the female that they are a fellow spider, and not a fly, by vibrating her web in a characteristic way. Others present the female with an insect that they have killed, so that, while her mouthparts are engaged in devouring his gift, he can mate with her in safety. Some male spiders tie up the female in a complex web of silk to prevent her attacking them.

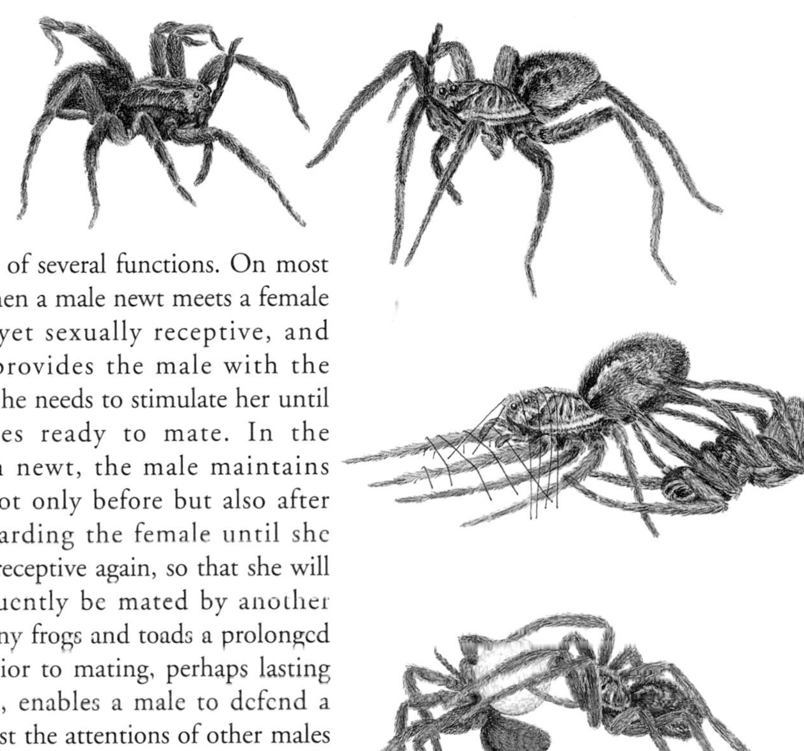

△ Aspects of courtship and mating in three species of spiders.
Top: The courtship signals of a male wolf-spider given before approaching the female.
Middle: The male crab spider, having fastened his mate to the ground with silk threads, is about to place sperm in her genital aperture.
Bottom: The male of the nursery web spider (right), presenting a wrapped prey to the female before mating.

△ *Although birds are fertilized internally, male birds have no penis. Male ducks and geese have a grooved organ down which sperm flow, but for most birds (such as these Arctic terns), copulation merely involves the male pressing his genital opening against the female's cloaca.*

Monogamous and polygamous females

For many female animals mating is a rare event, one insemination being sufficient to fertilize all of her eggs. For others, however, matings are frequent, sometimes with different males, sometimes with the same male. Multiple mating is a feature of the sexual behavior of many monogamous birds; pairs of ospreys, for example, mate several hundred times a day during the female's fertile period. This is not because females need to mate repeatedly to get enough sperm, or because mating is inefficient, but is related to the fact that females may occasionally mate with other males, in what are called extra-pair copulations. To maximize the chances that his partner's eggs are fathered by him, and not by another male, the male stays very close to his mate during her fertile period and courts and mates with her repeatedly.

In those insects in which the male's spermatophores contain nutrients, females may mate with several males to gain additional food. There are a number of other possible benefits that females may derive by mating with several males, including the production of genetically diverse offspring and insurance against the possibility that any one male is sterile. In birds that breed in groups containing more than one male, such as the dunnock, a female secures the cooperation of all the males in her group by mating with each of them. Because each may be the father of some of her progeny, it is in each one's interest to assist her in feeding and protecting her young.

Extra-pair copulations are only very rarely observed, both because they are relatively rare events and because females are typically very secretive when engaging in them. That they occur in many apparently monogamous species has been revealed in recent years by the new technique of DNA fingerprinting, which makes it possible to determine the exact paternity of each of a female's young. In the razorbill, birds are apparently monogamous, maintaining stable pairs that defend nest sites on cliff ledges. Away from the breeding colony, however, there are arenas where males gather and which females visit occasionally during their fertile period to mate with other males.

ALTERNATIVE MATING STRATEGIES

Where mating is highly competitive, most commonly because sexually active males greatly outnumber sexually receptive females, only some males can be successful if they adopt the typical pattern of mating of their species. In many animals this has led to the evolution of what are called alternative mating strategies—patterns of behavior by which males that are unsuccessful in competition achieve some degree of mating success by other means. In some frogs and toads, as in the natterjack toad, smaller males that cannot produce the louder, more rapidly-repeated calls that are preferred by females, abandon calling altogether. Instead, they sit near a larger, calling male and attempt to intercept females that are attracted to the calling male before they can reach him. Toads showing these alternative strategies are called "callers" and "satellites."

◁ *A small male natterjack toad takes up a position close to a larger one in order to take advantage of that male's ability to produce a louder mating call.*

Male bedbugs have a long, stiletto-like penis; rather than insert this into the female's genital opening, a male injects his sperm into her body by piercing her body wall. A male that has no mate will climb onto the back of one that does and use this device to inject his sperm into the genital tract of the mating male, who thus passes to the female sperm that are not his own!

◁ *Primarily monogamous animals sometimes mate frequently not just to ensure fertilization, but as a form of mate-guarding. Ospreys, for example, may copulate several hundred times each day during the female's brief fertile period, maximizing the chances that her offspring will be fathered by her mate and not by another male.*

Complicated mating rituals

In those frogs in which the eggs are looked after by one of the parents, mating and birth have become behaviorally complex because of the need to transfer the fertilized eggs to whichever parent is going to care for them. In the midwife toad, the male looks after the eggs. During mating, the strings of eggs become tightly wrapped around the male's hindlegs; he carries them about until they are ready to hatch, at which point he enters a pool so that the tadpoles can swim away. In the Surinam toad, the eggs develop in pockets in the skin on the female's back. In this species, mating involves a number of bizarre movements in which the pair, clasped tightly in amplexus, repeatedly turn over onto their backs so that the fertilized eggs fall onto the female's back. Mating is a lengthy process because only a few eggs at a time are produced, fertilized, and transferred to the female.

Some of the most complicated mating rituals are seen in animals that are hermaphrodites, that is, both male and female at the same time. In earthworms, slugs, and snails, ertilization is internal and mating involves the reciprocal exchange of sperm, each individual passing sperm to its partner. Earthworms lie alongside one another, pointing in opposite directions, so that their male and female genital openings are opposed to each other. During mating they hold themselves together by secreting a sticky sheath around their bodies. As this procedure has to be conducted on the ground surface, they are at great risk of being attacked by birds, so mating typically occurs at night.

In a hermaphrodite fish such as the black hamlet, two fish take it in turns to be male and female. One first plays the female role, producing a batch of eggs that are fertilized externally by the partner. Then their roles are reversed, and the other fish produces a batch for fertilization by the first. This alternation continues until both fish have used up all their eggs.

▽ *Earthworms, slugs, and snails are hermaphrodites, so mating involves the transfer of sperm from each animal's male reproductive organs to the other's female organs. Earthworms mate by lying parallel to each other, facing in opposite directions so their male and female genital openings are aligned, then secreting a sticky shroud that holds them together.*

△ *Incubation and birth are times of great risk for both mother and offspring. Some animals remain with their eggs or young for months at a time; others, such as cichlid fish, Surinam toads, and marsupial and stomach-breeding frogs, carry their eggs and young with them. Female wolf spiders protect their eggs and spiderlings in a silken sac, which they carry to protect them from predators.*

Giving birth

In animals with internal fertilization, mating and birth are separated in time, and giving birth is typically a much less spectacular event than in animals with external fertilization. In many reptiles, birds, and mammals, the female retires to the seclusion of a burrow, nest, or den to give birth to eggs or young, safe from predators. In many species the male plays a role in constructing and defending the birth place, and in some species females choose their mating partners on the basis of the quality of the sites they provide. In the American lark bunting, for example, females prefer to settle, mate, and breed in male territories that contain a lot of shade. In this species an important source of mortality among eggs is overheating by the sun, and territories with a lot of shade suffer lower egg-loss.

Females of a number of species synchronize their breeding activity so that they all give birth at very much the same time. In colonial sea birds, such as the herring gull, breeding synchrony yields a number of advantages. First, because a very large number of vulnerable chicks are all hatched at the same time, predators such as foxes are swamped by the sheer numbers, so that the risk to any one chick is greatly reduced. Second, if all females mate and lay their eggs at much the same time, it is very much less likely that males will be successful if, having mated with one female, they leave her and try to mate with another. With no receptive females available, the male's best strategy is to stay with his initial female and assist her to rear her young.

Mammals also often show breeding synchrony. Mating and birth are separated by the gestation period, during which the young develop and grow in the mother's uterus. There is evidence that some female mammals, such as the American bison, can shorten the gestation period so that they give birth at the same time as other females. This type of synchrony may be important for large, herbivorous mammals like the African wildebeest, which have to give birth out in the open rather than in a den because of its size and because so much of its time must be devoted to feeding. Wildebeest give birth during their annual mass migration and their young, born at an advanced stage of development, are able to run about and follow their mother within minutes of birth.

For animals that lay eggs, careful choice of a suitable egg-laying site may be vital to their reproductive success. Many insects whose larvae feed on plants must find and lay their eggs on the type of plant to which their larvae are specially adapted. Larvae of monarch butterflies, for example, are adapted to feed on the leaves of milkweed plants which are poisonous to most other animals. Dragonflies and damselflies lay their eggs on vegetation submerged just below the water surface.

When the female has specific requirements for egg-laying, it opens the way for males to enhance their mating success by defending those sites against rival males. Many male insects defend patches of food plants, and some dragonflies defend egg-laying sites, waiting for the females who must inevitably come there to lay their eggs.

△ ▷ *Social animals such as African wildebeest synchronize birth so a large number of young are born at the same time, spreading the risk from predators over as large a population as possible. Nevertheless, the weakened state of both mother and young makes this a vulnerable time.*

◁ *The reproduction of seabirds such as these blue-footed boobies is timed to coincide with the migration of the fish that are the main part of their diet. Mating, laying, and hatching take place within a few weeks, then one parent guards the chick against predators while the other catches fish, which is regurgitates into the chick's beak.*

Asexual Reproduction

A few animals are able to give birth to their young without mating at all. This is called asexual reproduction, and it takes a number of forms. In the small freshwater hydra, young are formed from buds that grow out of the side of the parent and then become detached as miniature adults. In a number of animals, including some fish, amphibians, and reptiles, but not birds or mammals, eggs can develop without being fertilized. This process is called parthenogenesis, meaning "virgin birth." In several parthenogenetic species, however, the fact that eggs develop without having to be fertilized by sperm does not mean that there is no form of interaction between males and females, despite the fact that, in such species, there are no males. In the Amazon molly, a small fish, females engage in courtship and mating with males of a very similar, sexual species. Their sperm do not fertilize the eggs but are necessary to initiate the process of cell division and development. Most remarkable is the behavior of the all-female, parthenogenetic whiptail lizard. Animals form courting pairs in which one lizard behaves like a female, the other like the male of a related, sexual species. It appears that, although these creatures do not require sperm to fertilize their eggs, they do require external stimulation of the kind provided by males in sexual species in order to complete the development of their eggs.

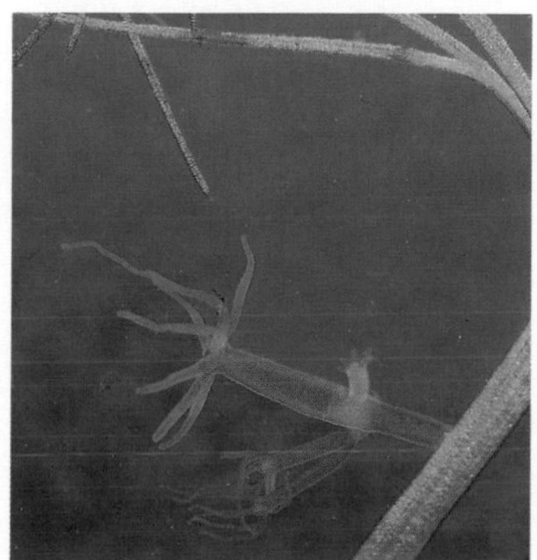

◁ *Freshwater hydra, which are common in streams and lakes around the world, range in size from species invisible to the naked eye to some that reach lengths of several millimeters. Their method of reproduction is asexual, in which fully formed miniature adults simply bud off the body of the parent.*

Rearing the Young

Terence Lindsey

Many animals go to extraordinary lengths to seek optimum circumstances for the sexual act itself, safe deposition of the eggs and, often, provision of food or safety for the young when they are born. But the notion of parenting, in the sense of direct individual care of a young animal after it has been born, is largely a vertebrate innovation. Here, the trend is toward more care invested in fewer, larger young, with a longer development period.

Post-laying care

Fishes and reptiles are rich in examples of post-laying care: the male of the South American lungfish, for example, goes to the extraordinary extreme of growing a set of supplementary gills on his pectoral fins, apparently the better to improve the oxygen supply to the eggs he guards in the turbid water of his underwater burrow. Many reptiles, including crocodiles, guard their clutches carefully and help the young hatch and reach the relative safety of the water. Social insects, and others such as earwigs, spend time caring for their young. Nevertheless, rearing the young is a class of behavior that reaches its greatest complexity in birds and mammals.

Though many reptiles guard their eggs, few incubate them. But almost all birds incubate their eggs. Once the eggs hatch, there is generally a period of dependence while the hatchlings develop the ability to fly.

Which parent will do the work?

The first element of parenting is deciding just which member of the pair will do it, and whether any "staff" are to be recruited to help. In birds, joint parenting is the norm, but in mammals there is a distinct trend to the mother playing the dominant role.

Almost 90 percent of all bird species are monogamous; that is, a single male unites with a single female to raise a brood of young. The pair-bond may last only for a single nesting attempt, as in many songbirds, or may last for life, as in some geese, parrots,

Above: This wedell seal pup will remain in his mother's care on the ice for two to three weeks and then in the water for several months, until it is ready to gradually leave its mother for longer periods and fend for itself in the open sea.

Left: Flamingos are about the most strongly social of birds, and breed together in large numbers. They invest in quality rather than quantity, raising one or two chicks a year.

△ *Many species of birds and mammals congregate to breed together in large numbers, sometimes, as in the Atlantic gannet, they do so with remarkable precision, almost all laying eggs, hatching and ultimately fledging at the same time.*

and albatrosses. Pairs often have helpers, and sometimes entire teams of auxiliaries. Trios are not unheard of, and either male or female may have multiple mates. Sometimes varies area to another, or sometimes from one individual to another.

In some species, all reproductive duties are more or less equally divided; in many others, the male helps in caring for the young but plays no part in nest-building or incubating the eggs. In some species, only the male incubates.

There are also many species in which the male takes no part whatever in nesting activities. These are often species in which the males congregate at display grounds, called leks, to attract females; females visit the lek, mate, and leave to nest and raise their young unaided. Contact is brief, and no pair-bond is formed. Such species include the birds-of-paradise, manakins, many hummingbirds, some grouse, and the ruff.

At the other extreme are several groups in which the female mates and lays eggs but otherwise contributes almost nothing to the rearing process. In phalaropes, for example, females are larger and more brightly colored than males, and take the initiative in courtship. The female mates, lays her eggs in a nest constructed by the male, then departs, leaving the male to incubate and raise the brood alone.

Megapodes

The megapodes (the word means "big-feet") are birds that do not incubate their eggs. Details vary between species, but the scrub-turkey is reasonably typical of the group. Upon reaching maturity, the male scrub-turkey establishes a territory in the forest and begins to build within it a mound of leaf litter, scraped together with long sweeping strokes of his big feet. Eventually he has a mound perhaps 3 ft (1 m) high and several feet across. This is now his mound, and he will spend the rest of his life tending it, defending it from other males, and never straying far from it.

Females do not build nests; instead, they approach the male's mound when ready to lay. If the mound is not ready to receive eggs, the male will chase her away; otherwise, he digs a hole in the mound, she lays her egg

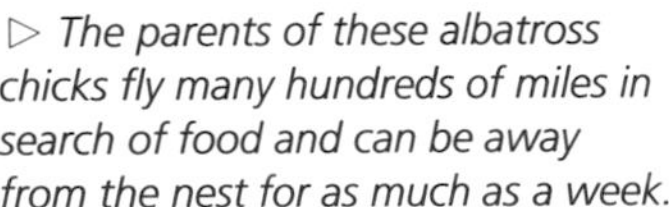

▷ *The parents of these albatross chicks fly many hundreds of miles in search of food and can be away from the nest for as much as a week.*

in it, he covers it over, and the female wanders off again into the forest. Further responsibility in the matter is entirely his.

Just like a heap of ordinary garden compost, the rotting vegetation deep within the mound gives off heat, and so begins and maintains incubation. In due course the eggs hatch, and the chick struggles to the surface and wanders off into the forest. Although there are a few reports of males offering some help in digging the chick free, even this is minimal, and there is no further parental care of any kind. Baby megapodes hatch in a more advanced state than any other bird, fully feathered and completely independent—chicks of some species can even fly a little.

△ In some cases, birds such as the white-winged chough of inland Australia live in permanent groups of eight to ten animals. When the dominant pair breed, all of the other members are involved in the care of the young hatchlings.

Precocial and altricial baby birds

The young of many familiar birds such as ducks and chickens are hatched in the form of bright-eyed fluffy little bundles that humans find extremely attractive. These youngsters cannot fly, but their eyes are open, and they can run nimbly within a few minutes of hatching. Not all birds hatch like this, and small songbirds, in particular, hatch naked, blind, and helpless, utterly dependent on their parents for warmth, food, and protection until they finally grow feathers after several weeks in the nest. Chicks of the first type are referred to as precocial, the second altricial. The same dichotomy is true of mammals: kittens, for example, are blind and helpless for some time, but the newborn of many antelopes can keep up with their mothers within a few minutes of birth.

Many details of the breeding cycle of birds can be seen in terms of exploiting various means of reducing the burden on the mother bird, and sharing it more equitably with the male parent. Males of many species feed their mates as part of the courtship ritual; in some species the male takes a turn at incubation; and in some groups of birds males even take over the entire burden of feeding the nestlings once they are hatched.

Let someone else do it!

Some birds do not build their own nests nor raise their own young; instead, they lay their eggs in the nest of some other bird, duping the rightful owners into raising the foreign egg as their own. This behavior is known as brood parasitism, and its most notorious practitioners include the cuckoos. All continents have representatives of the cuckoo family, though not all of its members are brood parasites—many build nests and raise their own young in the standard avian fashion. Representatives of several bird families unrelated to cuckoos also practice the habit, most notably the cowbirds of North America and the weavers of Africa.

In several cuckoos, the color and pattern of the eggs resemble those of the host species with

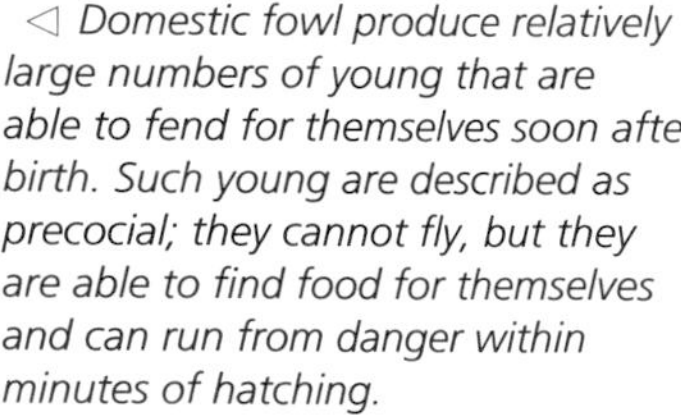

◁ Domestic fowl produce relatively large numbers of young that are able to fend for themselves soon after birth. Such young are described as precocial; they cannot fly, but they are able to find food for themselves and can run from danger within minutes of hatching.

HELPERS AT THE NEST

Many birds leave their parents' territories, or are forcibly ejected, a week or two after they fledge, and set out to establish their own territories and raise their own families. In many species, however, this does not happen. Youngsters may remain with their parents throughout their lives. Kookaburras patrol their territorial boundaries at dawn and dusk to call in groups in chorus with their neighbors, rather like howler monkeys in South American rainforests. About one-third of all adult kookaburras are "helpers," or non-breeding associates of established breeding pairs. Overall, these helpers contribute about one-third of the total time spent on incubating and brooding the eggs, and nearly two-thirds of all food delivered to nestlings.

Why do they not start families themselves? The reasons are complex and are only gradually becoming clear. Some environments may be so harsh and raising young in them so difficult, for example, that it simply doesn't pay an individual to waste time on the effort until it has had a good few years of practice at the task. Another possible reason is that, because with such help part of the burden of reproduction is lifted from the parents, they may be in a position to breed again more quickly—a significant advantage in environments prone to drought or flood—which enables the population to be rebuilt rapidly.

Whatever the reasons, a great number of bird species are now known to have helpers at the nest, almost always in the form of siblings of an earlier brood. This help ranges from brief and casual assistance to intricate, almost permanent involvement with the original nest.

The conclusion that helpers at the nest make a significant contribution to breeding success was dramatically reinforced when it was discovered that another Australian communally breeding bird, the white-winged chough, will sometimes form raiding parties to go out and capture "slaves" from neighboring family groups to come and help out when the indigent labor force is deemed inadequate.

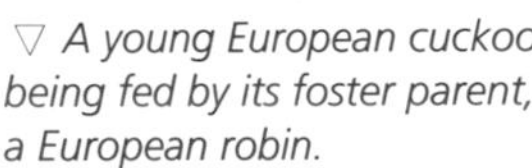

▽ *A young European cuckoo being fed by its foster parent, a European robin.*

remarkable fidelity, the better to dupe the parent hosts. But at this point it becomes significant whether the host builds an open, cup-shaped nest or a domed one—in the latter case it is dark inside the nest, and color and pattern play no part in duping the natural parent. Cuckoo species tend to specialize in either closed or open nests, seldom both.

When the typical female cuckoo is ready to lay an egg, she waits until a suitable target nest is unguarded (she has several possible candidates under surveillance at any one time), surreptitiously enters to lay her egg, then quickly slips away. She often removes or cracks one of the host's own eggs as she leaves. The host bird then returns and, unable to count, incubates her now augmented clutch in the normal way. The cuckoo egg usually hatches first, and the chick has an instinctive aversion to anything touching it. It struggles until any egg or chick sharing the nest has been ejected (some species have a depression in the back to facilitate the operation), thus commandeering the entire food supply delivered by its foster parents for itself. Many cuckoos are substantially larger than their hosts, and the foster parents often need to perch on their charge's head in order to feed it.

△ The provision of milk forges an extremely strong bond between mother and young. This European polecat will suckle her young for 30 days.

Mammalian milk

For rearing young, the supreme invention of the mammals is the development of special glands that produce and dispense a fluid expressly designed for the nurturing of the young, the mammary glands. A number of other animals in several groups produce nutritious material to feed their young, such as the crop secretions of most pigeons ("crop milk"), produced by both male and female and regurgitated to feed the chicks, and the even more bizarre secretions of the uterus in certain frogs and, possibly, the pouch of seahorses. But all of these systems lack the comprehensiveness and sophistication of the mammalian mammaries, in which the young is supported entirely on milk produced by the mother. Milk varies greatly in composition, both among various groups of animals and according to the growth stage of the infant. Apart from basic protein requirements, milk also provides the young with a balance of vitamins and minerals appropriate to its changing needs as it grows, and the system acts as an extension of the heavy investment in the young that is so characteristic of the vertebrates in general.

In some mammals, such as the grizzly bear, the supply of milk to the young is unconscious in the literal sense of the word: the young are born in the den while the mother is comatose during her winter sleep, and are suckled and grow for many weeks before the mother finally awakes in the spring.

◁ In many social animals, such as these Barbary macaques, the bond between parents and young is supplemented by the involvement of other members of the group, who also provide care for the young.

△ *Marsupials such as kangaroos give birth to their young at a very early stage, when they are minute in size. Immediately after birth, the embryo travels through the fur from the urogenital opening to the warmth and comfort of the mother's pouch, where it fastens itself to a teat and resumes development nourished by its mother's milk.*

Milk to suit all ages

In many of the kangaroos and wallabies, when a female gives birth she mates again almost immediately. However, the resulting fertilized ovum proceeds only a little way in its development, to a stage known as a blastocyst, and then stops. Its development is suspended by the mother's endocrine system, which is in turn influenced by the presence of the newborn youngster already in the pouch. The youngster suckling in the pouch may die or become lost, or it may leave normally as it nears independence (at about 230 days in the case of the red kangaroo); either way, the vacancy in the pouch acts as a signal to resume development of the stored blastocyst, a phenomenon referred to as delayed implantation. Estrus is not interrupted by pregnancy, and as the new youngster is born, mating takes place again. So a mature female effectively has a fertilized egg in reserve at all times. Not all kangaroos exhibit this feature: intriguingly, the eastern gray kangaroo does, but the closely related western gray kangaroo does not.

Kangaroos have evolved in an erratic environment in which lengthy droughts are interrupted by good seasons of unpredictable duration. Numbers accordingly fluctuate very widely, and it has been suggested that delayed implantation is a device that allows kangaroos to resume reproduction very rapidly when good times return after drought.

Kangaroos generally have four teats. Because there is some overlap in suckling a newborn young and completing the weaning process with its older sibling, lactation in some kangaroos has the extraordinary additional feature of delivering milk of different composition from different teats simultaneously—one teat is used by the newborn young, another by the "joey" being weaned.

Family life

Many vertebrate animals can be said to have virtually no family life at all. Marine turtles spend their entire lives with only casual and intermittent contact with their own kind. Several highly predatory mammals, such as the cougar and the snow leopard, are extremely solitary. Hunting over a very large home range, they go to some lengths to avoid direct contact with their neighbors.

Many other animals flock, although this is not necessarily anything more than a coming together at a common food supply. Many grazing mammals congregate in herds, but such gregariousness need not necessarily imply anything more than elementary

▷ *Lions hunt large prey that can only be brought down by complex cooperative hunting techniques. An important part of rearing their cubs is to teach them these strategies.*

anti-predator tactics. Any prey animal threatened by any predator can be thought of as being surrounded by a "domain of danger," and the animal can be expected to seek any means of reducing this domain. One of the simplest and most obvious ways of doing so is to take advantage of whatever shelter might be available behind a neighbor's own domain of danger—in other words, form a herd.

Nevertheless, the generally higher mental capacity of vertebrates over other animals makes ever more complex behaviors possible, and the advantages of complex behavior are best exploited in groups. Groups of individuals can interact in such a way as to reduce the investment in time or energy in a wide range of necessary activities such as guarding against predators, grooming, maintaining territories, or indeed catching prey. The complex interactions between individuals usually thought of as "family life" tend to reach their greatest diversity and richness among vertebrate animals, especially mammals.

Primate families

Often, a wide range of very different forms of social organization is evident among close relatives in a single group. Such a range is apparent in the primates—monkeys and apes.

As open country primates, baboons offer an example of family life for comparison with that of the great apes, which for the most part live in rainforests. Olive baboons inhabit the plains of East Africa, living in groups perhaps a hundred strong. Ranking is determined by the females: the oldest female generally has the highest seniority, followed by her daughters, then her most senior rival and her daughters, and so on down the line. Males are almost twice as big as females, yet a male can achieve status only by association with a female. He chooses a female and begins a process of ingratiation that may take several months; the

◁ △ ▽ *Primates such as Barbary macaques (left), ring-tailed lemurs (above) and olive baboons (below) carry their young with them. At the same time as giving constant care, it also provides them with vital lessons in social interaction, dealing with predators and food gathering.*

PEREGRINE SCHOOLDAYS

For most animals, parenting is pretty generally restricted to satisfying the obvious basic infant requirements of food, warmth, shelter, and protection from predators. But some must go further. In particular, predators need to invest relatively more than non-predators for an equivalent return in young successfully raised. Young predators must be taught to hunt. Peregrine falcons, for example, rely for food on sheer performance: they bring down their prey simply by outflying it. They prey almost exclusively on other birds, especially those ranging from about starling to pigeon in size. The standard hunting technique is to watch from some high exposed perch, scanning the sky for prey. The falcon then circles to a position high above the prey and kills or stuns it with a single devastating blow from an outstretched taloned fist as it hurtles past at the bottom of a spectacular 236 mph (380 kmph) dive.

Faced with such an attack, the victim may try to escape by heading for cover in a desperate high-speed dive of its own. But if the target is flying a little too low, the peregrine may fly below it, gradually forcing it higher and higher until it is too high to escape by diving and is committed to a straight chase for escape, whereupon the peregrine will then circle above to gain height for its swoop. Experienced peregrines can be extraordinarily efficient. Estimates are difficult because immatures need to be distinguished from adults and it is impossible always to be certain that the hunter is not merely practicing, but strike rates of a third to two-thirds seem routine. One male, nicknamed "The Red Baron" by researchers and kept under study for several years, sometimes scored 73–93 percent success rates, and had one remarkable run of 44 days in which he scored 68 kills without a single miss. Performance like this requires nuances of judgment that must be learned and practiced. Young peregrines spend two months in training after they fledge and before they leave their parents' territory, while the parents attempt to impart some of this performance by coaching and example. Adults lead young in mock chases, and drop prey from above for the young to catch; if it is missed, the other parent flying below may catch it and, swooping up and over the student, reposition it to drop again. The young practice on insects and other easy prey, and indulge in dog fights among themselves. Even with this training, the first few months alone are extremely difficult for a young peregrine, and the period of highest mortality lies between leaving the nest and the first birthday.

◁ *In developing their specialized hunting style, young peregrine falcons have to learn by observation and imitation if they are to hone their skills. Youngsters spend weeks under the tutelage of their parents, practicing on insects and other easy prey before they tackle larger birds.*

partnership is formed when she finally consents to be groomed by him. Life in a baboon troop is not quite so straightforward, however, because females often have several consorts, and it is not unusual for a male to partner several females—to such an extent that it has been suggested that the troop itself often has trouble keeping track of just who is dominant to whom.

Chimpanzees, in contrast, live in parties of very fluid composition, often loosely associated in communities that may range up to about 120 individuals. However, individuals feed, sleep, and often travel alone. Mating is promiscuous and sexual partnerships are seldom long-lasting. Males are somewhat more gregarious than females, and often form alliances with other males. Fighting is frequent because males freely move from group to group, so the make-up of a "gang" is seldom constant for long, and remembrance of past success or failure is little guide in predicting the outcome of any aggressive encounter.

Gorillas, on the other hand, live in close-knit, permanent communities headed by an old male, the silverback. Aggression is rare, and there is very little territorial defense. In contrast to almost every other social mammal, female gorillas leave their troop on reaching puberty, and the implication of this is that the females in any male's harem are unlikely to be related to each other, so the strongest bonds are between the silverback and each of his mates. Young males spontaneously leave the group from time to time, and may wander alone for years before joining other groups or establishing their own harem.

◁ *These black bear cubs learn many vital survival skills through play with their brothers and sisters. However, if the family is threatened, the mother quickly ushers her young cubs up a tree to safety.*

Finally, there is the orang-utan. Orang-utans contrast sharply with the other great apes in their all but non-existent social structures. By far the most solitary of the great apes, orang-utans seldom form more than temporary associations (apart from the mother-child relationship), and then normally only between adolescents. These apes inhabit rainforests of Borneo and Sumatra and feed mainly on fruit. They spend most of their time in the trees, and travel slowly and infrequently. Even when several come together at a fruiting tree or some similar site of temporary food abundance, there is little obvious social interaction at all, individuals merely arriving, gorging, then slipping quietly away when done.

But adult males, in particular, do have a strong sense of their spatial relationship to neighboring individuals, and it seems probable that the impressive "long call" of the male has at least a spacing function. In this announcement, a male first breaks off a branch and sends it crashing to the ground as an introduction to a series of loud bellowing roars, which reach a crescendo then die away in low bubbling groans. In this way, encounters between males are usually avoided and females can locate males when they are sexually receptive.

◁ *Orang-utans are the most solitary of the great apes, avoiding each other except during the breeding season. Even then, interactions are brief and casual, and the longest-lasting associations tend to be between a female and her infant or between adolescent orang-utans of both sexes.*

The pampered baby elephant

The element of education, or training, is the ultimate extension of the parenting process. Though many examples can be found among birds and even some reptiles, it reaches its most elaborate level among mammals.

Many of the largest mammals breed extremely slowly; a female gorilla, for example, averages only one young every six years. Elephants differ from other mammals in that they never entirely stop growing, although females slow markedly after about 25 years of age. Childhood is also an extremely lengthy process, and training merges almost imperceptibly into adult behavior.

Male and female elephants lead separate lives. Males are more or less solitary, but females live in close-knit groups of up to 25 individuals headed by an old matriarch. All are related, so any youngster born in the group is surrounded by adults who are its mother's sisters. Mutual bonds in the group are extremely strong. If there are several juvenile females in the group, almost all of the baby's daily needs apart from suckling may be supplied by these juveniles, known as allomothers or "aunties." One or other of them will guard it while it sleeps, pick it up if it falls down or gets stuck, fetch it if it strays, or come storming to the rescue if it should get into any kind of trouble. A baby elephant is treated by all members of its group with what often seems to human observers an extraordinary level of tolerance and indulgence. It is, in short, thoroughly spoilt.

A baby elephant can walk within an hour or two of birth, but reasonable proficiency in motor skills takes about three months. The finer points of trunk control take about three months longer. At three or four months the infant first tries to feed itself, and by the age of nine months vegetation is essential in the diet, but suckling often continues until the birth of the mother's next calf four or five years later.

It is difficult to draw any line between the care of the youngster in particular and the general level of mutual care within the group—the baby grows gradually from one into the other. In the case of a female calf, her aunts will be nearby to lend any reassurance or support that may be necessary at her first mating at around nine years of age. In elephants, the rearing process has a distinct endpoint only in the case of male calves,

△ *One of the strongest instincts young primates have is to follow their mothers lead, be it towards food, or out of danger. However, young elephants spend as much time in the care of "aunties" (other adult females) as they do with their own mothers.*

◁ *(Far left) Much of an elephant's infancy and adolescence are spent learning about living in the extended family into which they are born, in an atmosphere of what to humans seems extraordinary tolerance and indulgence. This environment of strong, mutual care is a conspicuous characteristic of elephant society.*

FOOD AND SHELTER

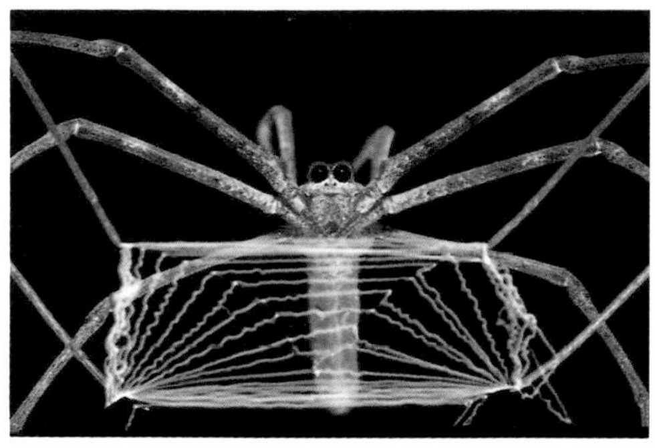

HUNTING

Dr. Joshua R. Ginsberg and Danielle Clode

The term "hunting" conjures up images of a stealthy predator lurking in the undergrowth, approaching its prey closer and closer until, with a lightning burst of speed, the hunter strikes, bringing down its unsuspecting prey.

This image incorporates, in simplified form, the basic components of a hunt: searching, stalking, and capture. The way in which different animal hunters have adapted and diversified this basic predatory pattern is, however, remarkable. Animals employ a surprising array of strategies and techniques to efficiently gain themselves a meal of recently live flesh.

Hunters face the unique pressure of having to capture food that, once alerted to the presence of the hunter, often moves away as rapidly as possible. The evolutionary history of a predatory species is one of continual adaptation and improvement of strategies designed to outwit the unwilling victim. In response, prey species have evolved a wide variety of anti-predator strategies: some have grown bigger; some have grown smaller; others have found strength in numbers and evolved to live in groups; some have acquired weapons of their own, such as sharp horns; while other species have become more alert, or faster, or both. Many prey species adopt a mixture of these strategies. Predator-prey evolution becomes, in a sense, an arms race. For the predator, staying one step ahead of the prey is critical for survival.

Keeping one step ahead of the prey

The great diversity of animal hunting strategies can be divided into two main groups: solitary and cooperative hunters. Solitary hunters have usually evolved specialized techniques to help them catch prey and kill it quickly while avoiding either losing

Above: The female of the Australian net-casting spider spins a net from its own silk, waiting in ambush for night-flying moths so that it can enfold them with a sudden, spreading cast of its sticky snare.

Left: The classic image of a hunter is that of the lion, which stalks its prey then attacks in a sudden, leaping rush that has been timed at 200 feet (60 m) per second.

△ *Lions hunt cooperatively or individually, depending on the type of habitat, the type of prey, and other factors. Curiously, stalking and hunting in a group does not offer any greater guarantee of success than solitary tactics.*

▽ *No matter whether prey has been captured by a single lioness or by all the adult members of the pride working together, the meal is shared with the males, who play little part in hunting, sauntering in to take, literally, the lion's share.*

the beast they are trying to kill or being injured in the process of hunting. These techniques include injecting poison into a prey item or increasing the speed and efficiency of the killing bite to rapidly immobilize the prey.

Animals which hunt cooperatively usually join forces with members of their own or other species—and occasionally with human beings. The evolutionary prerequisite for communal hunting is that each individual is more successful when hunting in a group than when hunting alone. As in solitary hunting, there are various methods cooperative hunters employ. While some species overwhelm their prey by the sheer force of numbers, other cooperative hunters improve their killing rate by having individuals within the group adopt different hunting techniques, including taking up different positions in the hunting party.

The prowess of the lion

The archetypal cooperative hunter is the lion. This matriarchal social felid is unique among the cats for its sociality and cooperation in hunting large game. Lions live in large family groups with up to 18 closely related females and their cubs and one to five males. The group revolves around the females, who do the great majority of the hunting. Males hunt less frequently, preferring to let the females do the work then sauntering in after the kill.

Hunting in groups allows lions to take prey much larger than themselves. Oddly, despite this highly evolved hunting strategy, individual lions do not always eat more when hunting in groups (a full belly being the best measure of hunting success!). Hunting success appears to be related to a wide variety of factors: group size, habitat type, the season of the year, and the prey type available. In Uganda, for instance, lions appear to have greater hunting success in groups only when hunting in tall grass; in the open, where their encircling strategy is bound to fail, group hunting doesn't work as well. In the Serengeti National Park in Tanzania, group hunters do better than solitary hunters only in the wet season when grass is high and larger prey is available.

Killer whales

Coordinated group hunting, although best studied in lions, is seen in many species. In the oceans, "pods" or groups of orcas, also known as killer whales, have become specialists in group hunting efforts. Orcas, like lions, live in matriarchal societies with pod sizes of two to 12 animals.

Orcas hunt a variety of prey, including whales, dolphins, and seals. Hunting is a coordinated affair; perhaps the most spectacular example is when they chase and attack a large baleen whale. Some orcas fling themselves on top of the whale to impede its breathing, others harass it from the front to prevent it from diving deep, still others bite at its flippers and body. Eventually, the orcas overwhelm their prey and, in a feeding orgy, tear chunks of meat off the whale.

△ Orcas specialize in cooperative hunting. While an experienced orca charges an unsuspecting sealion pup at the edge of the surf, other members of the pod wait offshore to snare any animal that escapes.

Living "fishing nets"

Schooling prey seems especially suitable for predation by cooperation. Although the individual prey types vary, the technique for hunting schooling prey is remarkably similar across species. The techniques involve three stages: circling or cutting off avenues of escape; concentrating prey into a tighter target; and attack. Groups of dolphins concentrate their prey by herding schooling fish into shallow waters—surrounded, and unable to flee down into the water column, the fish are easily picked off by the dolphins.

Seabirds also cooperate to increase their hunting success. Blue-eyed cormorants form huge "rafts" of birds over schools of fish. The rafts dive in unison, maximizing the confusion in the school they are attacking; in the confusion, each cormorant eats its fill. Pelicans, in contrast to the cormorant frenzy, sedately encircle a school of fish, drawing the school into a more tightly bunched group as if they were being concentrated in a slowly closing purse-seine fishing net. Once the school is concentrated, the pelicans simultaneously scoop the tightly packed fish into their pouched beaks.

Even crocodiles, usually portrayed as scavengers and lone hunters of large animals, apparently cooperate to catch fish. The Nile crocodile gathers in groups in areas where water flow is restricted to a single outlet. This pattern of water flow forces fish down the river straight into the jaws of the crocodiles. The crocs form a semi-circle around this one-way fish flow to reduce the chances of fish escaping between two crocodiles. Moving from its position might, in the short term, increase an individual's catch, but in the long term the cooperative crocodiles catch more of the fish moving downstream than a solitary hunter could.

▽ While crocodiles use a variety of individual and cooperative hunting strategies, including ambush and sudden, charging attacks, to capture prey, they are naturally ready to take advantage of a ready-made meal in the form of a drowned zebra or wildebeest.

UNITED THEY KILL

The cooperative exploitation of prey already concentrated by a natural force can be seen in several species, including such usually solitary birds of prey as the falcons. A spectacular example of this is seen in Eleanora's falcon of Paximada, an island off Crete in the Aegean Sea. The falcons form a huge wall stretching upward as far as the eye can see, blocking the path of small birds migrating from Europe to Africa. Such cooperation between the males of different nesting pairs is unusual and may arise coincidentally as each male takes up a prime hunting spot, close to his nest, yet not too close to another male. More typically among most animals, cooperation occurs within a small family unit, as seen in otters, lions, and orcas. An avian example of such cooperation is seen in Harris's hawk. These hawks form small groups of two or three birds which soar across their feeding range, keeping within sight of other similarly formed small groups. Once a prey item, such as a rabbit, is sighted, the small group of hawks may employ one of a number of strategies. Like lions, a number of hawks may converge on the rabbit from different directions, confusing its choice of escape route. Or, like wild dogs hunting in the open plain (see box "Running with the Pack" on page 55), the hawks may take up a relay attack, with each bird in the group taking its turn to chase the rabbit intensively until it is exhausted. Like the wild dogs, the hawks use a different strategy should the rabbit take cover in thick vegetation. One or two hawks may land and, like beaters taking part in a hunt, flush the prey from its hideout, enabling the other birds in the group waiting outside to capture it. These strategies enable the small hawks to capture rabbits which can be substantially larger than themselves.

△ *Despite their speed and formidable talons, birds of prey can only kill or carry large prey when it is completely exhausted. Harris's hawks hunt in groups of two or three to harry a rabbit, for example, until it is so confused and spent that it can be attacked and killed.*

▽ *Chimpanzees sometimes use the unusual strategy of picking up and throwing stones at their prey.*

Learning to hunt

Cooperative hunting can be important to species in which young animals need to learn hunting skills from their elders. Killer whales demonstrate this dramatically with the hunting technique involving intentional stranding to catch prey on beaches. Orcas capture seals in the surf on breeding beaches of Patagonia and islands in the southern Indian Ocean. The whales surge up the beach and capture an unsuspecting elephant seal. They then fling themselves backward off the beach, prey in jaw, using the receding waves to help propel them back into the ocean. This intentional stranding is also seen in play behavior of the orca. An adult will often strand itself on a beach in the company of a juvenile, even when no seals are present. At other times, the adult orca will toss a dead seal to a juvenile that has play-stranded on the beach. The process teaches the young orcas how to employ this unusual hunting strategy.

The learned acquisition of hunting behavior may also occur in our closest relative, the chimpanzee. For years, scientists assumed that the chimp was essentially a vegetarian. But chimpanzees are effective communal hunters. Young chimpanzees frequently accompany adults when they go out to hunt smaller monkeys and small forest ungulates, although adult males are most successful at capturing the prey. Hunting in groups, and using the same circling and chasing strategies as many other animals, chimpanzees are unusual in that they throw stones to startle or flush prey.

Mixed-species communal hunting

In theory, communal hunting should evolve when the process of cooperation allows each hunter to do better in a group than it would on its own. The best confirmation of this theory is that cooperation is not limited to members of the same species. Some social species, whose complex interactions with their own kind predispose them to interpreting the behavior of others and coordinating their own efforts with those of others, hunt cooperatively with other species.

Cormorants and pelicans may circle a school of fish together, the cormorants benefiting from the herding action of the pelicans and the pelicans benefiting from the cormorants diving under the school of fish and preventing the fish from escaping below. Snowy egrets aggregate on the river edge where pied-billed grebes have driven in shoals of fish. The egrets and their stabbing beaks prevent the fish from taking refuge along the banks; the grebes scoop up under the egrets and grab the fish.

But the association of two species in a hunting effort does not always benefit both parties. Fishing ducks, such as pied-billed grebes, may also drive fish inshore for the waiting egrets, yet they are too large to fish underneath the egrets and reap the benefits of the egrets' fishing technique.

Of men, dolphins, and whales

The chain of hunting behavior, and the behavior of the hunted, can become quite complex, involving a number of different species. At times, seabirds are seen feeding on small fish which are being chased by tuna. In turn, the tuna are being pursued by dolphins. Into this melée step the fishermen, who in turn are attracted by and attract a feeding frenzy of birds, fish, and sea mammals. In some cases this association has led to dolphins being killed in the nets of the fishermen, but the association can also result in cooperation between the dolphins and the fishermen.

The history of this cooperation is ancient, with reports dating back to Roman times. Dolphin–human fishing cooperation is still practiced in areas as widely separated as Africa and South America. Vast schools of migrating mackerel close to shore are spotted by the waiting fishermen who "call" the dolphins by beating the surface of the water rapidly. This sound actually imitates the noise of a mackerel school being pursued, as they leap out of the water to escape. The fishermen set their nets in a semi-circle facing out to sea; the activity of the dolphins drives the fish shoreward into the nets.

In the recent past, humans have also hunted cooperatively with orcas off the southeast coast of Australia. In particular, the whalers of Twofold Bay, New South Wales, developed a complex hunting arrangement with their local orca population. Whenever a large baleen whale was located off the coast, a member of the orca pod would come into the harbor. Alerted by the orca, the whalers would take their small

△ ▽ *Animals of different species sometimes hunt cooperatively, especially when large numbers of prey are available. Pelicans and cormorants (above) often use this strategy: the cormorants benefit from the pelicans' herding of the school, and the pelicans from the cormorants diving beneath the fish and driving them to the surface. Dolphins (below) cooperate with fishermen—and sometimes with sharks—to herd schools of fish. Tuna fishermen locate their catch by observing seabirds feeding on small fish being hunted by tuna ... which are in turn being hunted by dolphins.*

craft out of the bay and harpoon the whale. The orcas would grasp the cables and drag the whale underwater to drown it. The whalers returned to shore, and the whale carcass would later drift ashore minus the tongue—the orcas' reward for their part in the hunt. This association went on for 80 years, until the 1930s, during which time the individual members of the pod became well-known and many of the orcas had sheared their front teeth through from grasping the wire cables.

When enemies become friends

Not all hunting associations involve naturally cooperative species. The usually solitary ratel or honey badger of Africa operates in conjunction with goshawks to hunt rodents. The keen-eyed goshawks frequently hover low over the burrow where a rodent has taken cover, unable to excavate it. The ratel takes advantage of this cue and lumbers over to dig beneath the goshawk. It catches some of the rodents while the goshawk picks off fleeing animals that are too quick for the ratel.

In North America, two predators which usually compete for prey have worked out an association to improve their hunting success. The solitary badger is sometimes found hunting for small mammals in association with a coyote. The badger unearths rodents —which are usually out of the reach of the coyote—by digging with its strong front limbs; the coyote catches the animals that sneak past the badger. In return for the badger's efforts, the sharp-sighted coyote locates prey at a greater distance than might the badger on its own. The coyote also keeps vigil for other predators and scavengers while the badger is busy digging. Although the badger and coyote do cooperate, their relations are not always so genial. Badgers have been known to eat coyote pups, while a pack of coyotes may prey on a lone badger.

△ ▷ Although the North American badger (above) is notoriously solitary and short-tempered, it occasionally cooperates with coyotes (right). The badger excavates a rodent burrow while the coyote catches any animals that evade the badger's jaws; in return, the coyote deters scavengers and other predators, and sometimes leads the badger to other food sources.

Softly, softly

Cooperative hunting is not the only solution to overpowering large prey. Solitary hunters can simply become larger themselves. The largest of the cats, the tiger, is primarily a solitary hunter relying first on stealth and surprise, and then on sheer weight to fell its victims on impact before killing with a suffocating bite.

The largest of the land carnivores is also a solitary hunter. The nomadic polar bear of the northern icecaps uses not only sheer size, but also many different hunting strategies which require much skill to master. Young polar bears spend two years with their mother, carefully mimicking her hunting behavior and learning the importance of a stealthy approach. Only fully grown polar bears are heavy enough to break through the ice covering the frozen dens of seals to prey on seal pups. So a more common strategy is the "still" hunt: waiting absolutely motionless on the edge of a breathing hole in the ice, then smashing the skulls of the unsuspecting seals with a blow of the forepaw as they surface. Not surprisingly, given their ferocity and their history of man-eating, polar bears are shown great respect by people living and working in the Arctic.

The polar bears' counterpart in southern waters is the lithe and sinuous leopard seal. Reaching lengths of up to 10 ft (3 m), it is capable of outswimming and outmanoeuvering most of its prey, usually seals and penguins, but it too prefers to wait for its prey rather than pursue it. Its ominous presence beneath the ice floes causes great anxiety among the penguins, who nervously huddle at the edge of the ice, unwilling to be the first to dive. Eventually, the sheer mass of bodies crowding at the edge pushes the first unfortunate few in. Staying out of the water is no guarantee of safety, as leopard seals can track penguins from beneath the clear Antarctic ice, their reinforced skulls enabling them to burst through the ice to capture a penguin.

△ *The leopard seal lies in wait at the edge of the ice shelf to catch penguins as they enter or leave the water, or stalks both penguins and smaller seals from beneath the ice, through which it breaks to seize its prey.*

◁ *Polar bears are solitary hunters, lying motionless by a seal's breathing hole, then leaping forward to scoop the unsuspecting seal out of the water with a paw. Adult bears also use their keen sense of smell to locate the ice-covered dens containing seal pups, then use their weight to break in.*

△ ▽ *Humans idealize lions and tigers for their supposed courage, yet abjure other predators that behave in the same way. Cobras (above) are responsible for thousands of deaths a year throughout Asia, but are treated with respect and even affection, largely because of their role as killers of rodent pests. The great white shark (below) is hated and feared as a "man-eater," though it is responsible for no more than three or four attacks on humans each year.*

Crocodiles and sharks

Another large predator, the saltwater crocodile, relies on stealth to get within striking distance of its prey—usually a medium-sized mammal. Watching its intended victim for days beforehand, learning its routine, the crocodile waits for precisely the right moment. A second of vulnerability and the crocodile strikes, dragging its meal underwater to drown.

Little is known about the largest of all living hunters, the sperm whale, although it is thought to feed on giant squid inhabiting depths of over 3,000 feet (900 m). Our only account of battles that must be of truly gargantuan proportions, are the welts of huge squid suckers scarring the corpses of sperm whales taken by whalers.

The great white shark shares with the large crocodiles an unpleasant reputation for killing humans. Crocs and great whites are among the few "man-eating" species not to have been mercilessly culled by humans—but this is not for want of trying. Indo-pacific crocodiles were in fact in danger of extinction before protective legislation was introduced in Australia in 1974. Similarly, sharks face unending persecution from "great white hunters," and are perhaps only spared decimation because of their secretive habits as youngsters. Very few small great white sharks—under 12 ft (4 m)—are ever seen; it is thought that at this fish-eating stage of their lives they eschew the company of larger great white sharks, which can grow to over 20 ft (6.5 m) and are likely to eat them. Any warm seal-sized object is a meal to a white shark as it uses its sensitive sense of smell to find its food. Sharks of this family must surely rank among the most unsociable of the vertebrates, with the live-born young frequently eating each other while still inside the mother.

Giant-killers

As a general rule, hunting large prey requires either cooperative hunting effort or large body size. But not all animals conform to this rule, most notably the small mustelids; weasels, stoats, ferrets, and mink frequently tackle prey up to five times their own body weight. With small prey the mustelids, like the small cats, deliver a precise killing bite to the neck, severing the spinal cord. Stoats employ the same tactics

on large prey such as rabbits, despite the fact that this does not actually kill the prey. In fact, it seems that some animals simply die of fright from being attacked by such a tenacious little predator.

Once they are attached to their prey, nothing can induce these mustelids to let go until their victim stops moving: weasels have been carried off in flight by large birds, and a mink would rather be pulled from its den by an irate poultry farmer than relinquish its freshly caught chicken.

Poisoning the prey

Another strategy for animals wanting to kill prey much larger than themselves is to chemically immobilize the prey before attacking. The best known examples of this are the poisonous snakes—hundreds of species around the world use this strategy to capture their prey, and as a form of self defense.

The cobra family belongs to a group of poisonous snakes, the elapids, which have fangs at the front of their mouths. When they strike, cobras throw their head forward and downward, the front fangs stabbing the prey and releasing the venom.

◁ ▽ *Some animals hunt prey that is not only as large as or larger than themselves, but that is also predatory and capable of killing and eating the hunter. Scorpions, spiders, wasps, and other venomous invertebrates, as well as many snakes—even at least one species of shrew—inject venom into their prey to kill or immobilize it.*

Cobras use neurotoxins—chemicals which affect the nervous system and result in paralysis, nausea, shortness of breath, and eventual suffocation. In some cases, heart failure leads to the immediate death of the prey.

Spiders, scorpions, and wasps avoid the risk of injury from their large prey by injecting toxins which rapidly immobilize or kill the victim.

Only a few primitive mammals possess the capacity to produce poisons. The highly endangered shrew-like solenodon of the West Indies is one such mammal. Solenodons presumably use their toxic saliva to immobilize their prey.

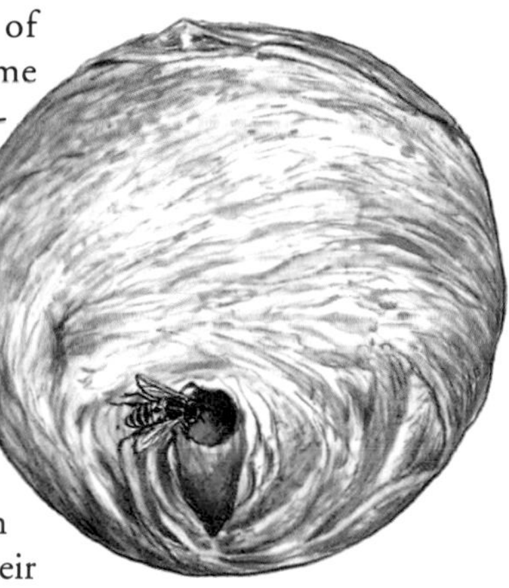

THE KILLING BITE

Small cats dispatch their prey with a rapid killing bite, yet this lightning speed disguises the sophisticated range of adaptations required for this technique. Their sharp canine teeth are precisely the right width to insert between the vertebrae of their prey and sever the spinal cord. This minute gap can be felt by teeth well provided with nerves with a few exploratory bites. Powerful jaw muscles control the shortened and curved mandible, enabling a deep stabbing strike and a quick death.

The small cats' remaining teeth are especially adapted to slicing flesh, and their rough tongues enable meat to be stripped from the bone.

While the small cats rely on a quick clean kill, the less efficient mustelids (which also employ a neck bite) have developed massive neck muscles to maintain their grip on struggling victims. These victims may take some time to die of exhaustion, loss of blood, or fright.

◁ △ *Predatory small mammals often have to handle prey larger than themselves. While cats employ a rapid, disabling bite between the neck vertebrae to sever a victim's spinal cord, mustelids such as weasels and ermines have greatly enlarged neck muscles to enable them to hang on to a struggling animal until it can be suffocated or overpowered.*

STALKERS AND SPITTERS

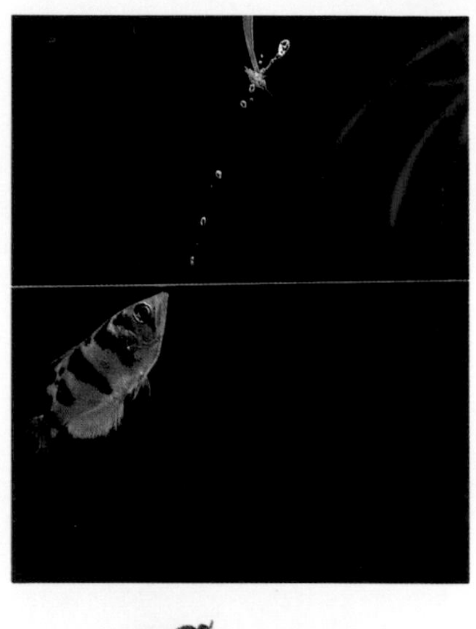

Most spiders use a web to capture their prey although some, such as the wolf spiders of the Lycosidae family, stalk. Yet even among the web-weaving spiders, not all are passive feeders awaiting food to fly their way. The bolas spiders of Australia lower a sticky globule of silk containing a potent brew of pheromones mimicking that of female moths. As the male moths flutter about vainly searching for the elusive mate, the spider begins to swing the treacherous drop back and forth until it collides with an orbiting moth. This is not the only sticky end that can befall the unsuspecting invertebrate. The spitting spider ejects a droplet of glue up to an inch (2.5 cm), sticking its prey in its tracks.

Such projectile weaponry is not confined to spiders. The archer fish of Australasia captures prey outside its aquatic realm by squirting water at insects, dislodging them from overhanging twigs. Ant lions of the Myrmeleiontidae family also dislodge their prey by throwing things at them. These larval predators dig themselves into a steep pit in fine sand; any passing ants falling into the pit have difficulty climbing out. The ant lion moves sand at the bottom of the pit, causing an avalanche, or throws grains of sand at the clambering insect, resulting in it sliding down into waiting jaws.

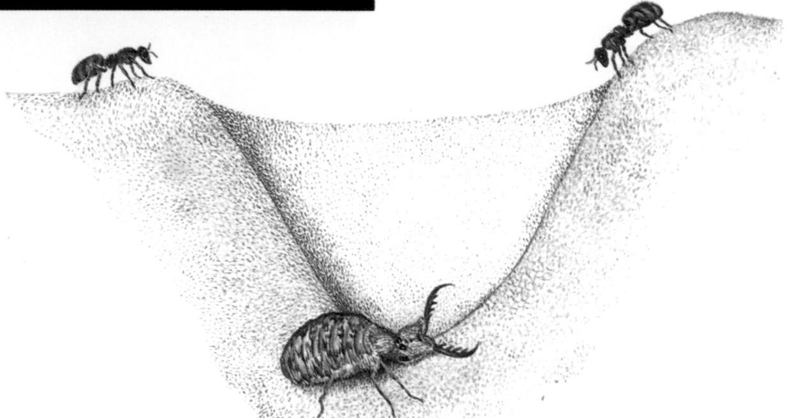

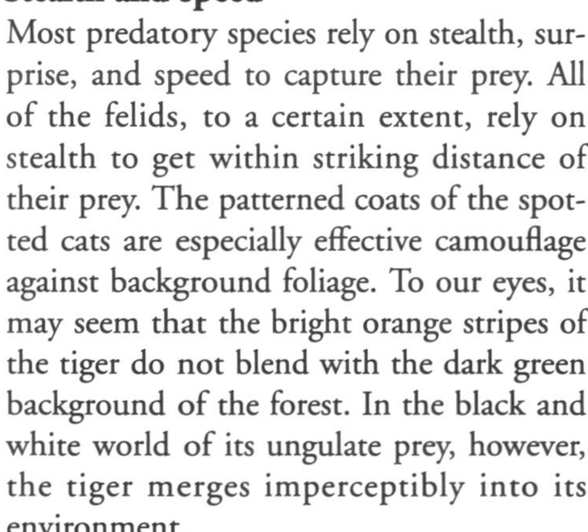

◁ The archer fish (above left) of Australia and New Guinea spits a stream of water droplets to dislodge insects from leaves or twigs overhanging the water. In similar fashion, the ant lion (left) digs a sloping pit into which ants and other insects wander; when it detects a potential meal, the ant lion directs a stream of sand grains that causes its prey to tumble into its waiting jaws.

Stealth and speed

Most predatory species rely on stealth, surprise, and speed to capture their prey. All of the felids, to a certain extent, rely on stealth to get within striking distance of their prey. The patterned coats of the spotted cats are especially effective camouflage against background foliage. To our eyes, it may seem that the bright orange stripes of the tiger do not blend with the dark green background of the forest. In the black and white world of its ungulate prey, however, the tiger merges imperceptibly into its environment.

This combination of stealth and speed appears again and again in the predatory world. Different species of praying mantid have evolved a bewildering array of plant-like bodies. This enables them to hide on the vegetation before striking, in less than one twentieth of a second, at the unwary prey. The chameleon changes its skin color to blend with the surrounding vegetation, its movements imperceptibly slow until, faster than the human eye can behold, its sticky tongue impales its prey.

But by far the master of the multicolored coat is the cuttlefish. Like most cephalopods, its skin is a kaleidoscope of ever changing patterns used both to communicate and to conceal. By mimicking its background the cuttlefish can approach its prey closely, as any solitary stealthy hunter might, but suddenly it becomes a mesmerizing mass of shifting colors and patterns before striking its confused prey at close range.

Wolves in sheep's clothing

Not all species are fortunate enough to be born with powers of concealment. Some, such as the assassin bug nymph, have to work at it. These nymphs eat termites, but the termite mound is guarded by ferocious soldiers who attack and expel anyone who fails to carry the smell of the colony. The assassin bug nymph becomes a "wolf in sheep's clothing" by coating itself with the scent-impregnated sand of the colony and with the corpses of its unfortunate victims.

More commonly, predators will use some part of their own body to mimic the food of their prey. Many aquatic predators, for instance, have appendages that look like tasty, wiggling morsels to a hungry fish. Too late, the fish discovers that it has swum right into the mouth of a predator such as an alligator snapping turtle lying part buried in the mud. In the darker realms of the deep sea such lures may be lit—the angler fish, for instance, dangles a lantern on a pole in front of its mouth, enticing meals out of the gloom.

Back on land, the green heron has no such fancy fishing tackle but uses insects, feathers, or bits of food as lures to attract fish to the surface. Carefully depositing its lure upstream, the heron then watches intently as it passes by. If the lure fails to attract the attention of a fish, it is retrieved before it passes out of reach and is repositioned upstream. Other birds have also been recorded as using lures in this fashion, including the pied kingfisher, the sun bittern, and even a black kite.

◁ *Almost indistinguishable from the stream-bottom mud in which it hides, the snapping turtle of tropical and sub-tropical North America beguiles fish, frogs—and smaller turtles, including members of its own species —with a wriggling, worm-like lure in its lower jaw.*

◁ *Although the cheetah is famed as the world's fastest land animal, capable of running at speeds of 75 mph (120 kph), it relies on its tawny, spotted coloration to blend in to the savannah, enabling it to get close enough to its prey for a sprinting attack.*

▽ *Tropical praying mantids can be almost indistinguishable from the flowers of the trees they inhabit, perhaps attracting flower-visiting insects to them.*

△ *Lacking powerful natural weapons, speed, or other advantages, humans have relied for their success on their ability to manipulate their environment. This includes taking advantage of other animals' abilities, from using dogs for hunting to exploiting otters' fishing skills in China and Pakistan.*

▽ *Falconry probably began when wild birds of prey followed humans and dogs on hunting trips. Beginning as an efficient means of catching fast-moving prey such as rabbits, pigeons, and other game birds, falconry persists as a sport in the Middle East.*

Humans and hunters

Humans have commandeered the hunting capacities of many species to acquire food and control pests. Some species, such as the cat, have remained independent of human control despite being domesticated. Similarly, ferrets, although used to hunt rabbits since Roman times, have remained very similar to their wild forebears, the polecats.

But the fate of many other species has become inextricably intertwined with that of humans. Of the carnivores, dogs have been bred for hunting in various guises since at least 645 BC, when mastiffs in a hunting party were depicted on the walls of the palace of Ashurbanipal in Nineveh. It seems likely that dogs were initially attracted to human settlements to scavenge. The complex social behavior of dogs enabled hand-reared pups to accept the human family as dominant members of its pack. No doubt they were used as guard dogs to protect livestock from the depredations of their wild cousins. By the time of the Roman Empire, a variety of dogs from small lap dogs to large hunting dogs were being bred.

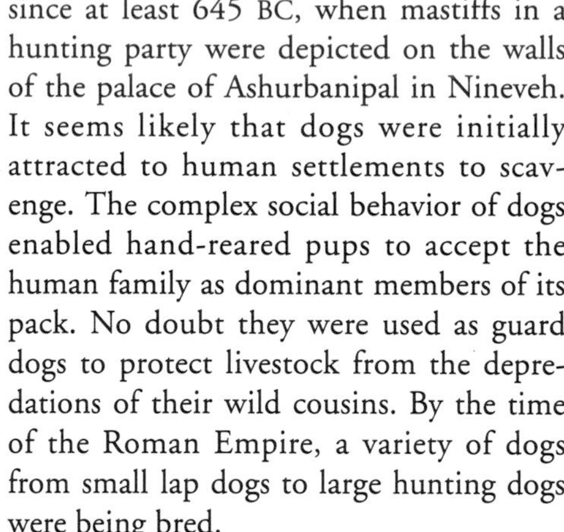

Not all species have proved so malleable to human interests, however. From the fifteenth century until the eighteenth century, Indian royalty found the use of cheetahs to hunt game very successful. This species had first been used by the Ancient Egyptians and Assyrians. The cheetah was released close to a herd of deer and after a short chase brought down the kill, or returned of its own accord to its cage empty-handed. Despite the royal treatment of successful hunters, cheetahs did not become household pets—largely because of the difficulty in breeding them in captivity.

Similarly, the use of otters to catch fish in China proved less enduring than a more successful fishing partnership with cormorants. In the latter case, a collar is usually fitted around the bird's neck to prevent large fish from being swallowed, and a cord with a float is attached to its leg. The technique ranges from a solitary fisherman shuffling neck-deep through the water with one bird on his shoulder, to flotillas of rafts with up to 100 birds fishing inside a circled net.

This traditional fishery even caught on as a craze for the wealthier European classes in the seventeenth and eighteenth centuries. No doubt this stemmed from their ongoing fascination with falconry. Wild raptors will often follow hunts, such as grouse shoots, where wounded or flushed birds can be picked off easily. It is probable that this early association of the birds of prey with human hunters led to the taming of young birds and their eventual use as hunters of rabbits, pigeons, and game birds.

◁ Baleen whales, such as the humpback whale, which feed by filtering millions of small shrimp-like crustaceans known as krill, do not appear to be likely hunters. But they are not just the victims of cooperative hunting by orcas. Krill are frequently thinly dispersed throughout the water. Humpbacks use a technique known as "bubbling" to round up schools of krill into dense clouds. Several humpbacks circle below a school of krill, gradually releasing a trail of air bubbles that rise to the surface, causing the krill to move into the center. The circle is tightened as the humpbacks rise until, approaching the surface, the humpbacks scoop through the school, their massive mouths breaking the surface of the water in unison.

Running with the Pack

Most wild members of the dog family are small solitary hunters. Animals such as foxes and jackals specialize in killing mice, rats, and even large insects for their dinner. In contrast, however, the larger pack-living canids—the African wild dog, the Asian dhole, and the wolf—are among the most cooperative of social hunters. Most foxes and jackals live in monogamous pairs, raising two or three pups each year. Larger canids, such as the black-backed jackal, the coyote, the dingo, or the highly endangered Ethiopian wolf, live in extended families including yearling animals which remain with their parents to help raise the new litter of brothers and sisters. This extended social group is closely linked with the evolution of communal hunting. In most circumstances, these animals continue to hunt small prey like rodents. But when larger prey are abundant, dingoes will abandon the marsupial rat diet and hunt kangaroos, coyotes will leave behind their spiky porcupine diet for white-tailed deer, and the Ethiopian wolf will chase mountain nyala calves in preference to giant mole rats.

In the open plains of the Serengeti National Park, in Tanzania, a pack of African wild dogs will cover huge areas, up to 580 square miles (930 sq km) in a single year. In these huge areas, small prey like Thomson's gazelle, 20–50 lb (10–20 kg), may at times be abundant, while at other times large prey, including wildebeest and zebra, will dominate a pack's hunting area. It is not uncommon for larger canids to switch prey preference when the availability of favored food species changes.

The African wild dog is known for its endurance and persistence. In the open plains of the Serengeti/Masai Mara, the dogs spread out in a phalanx and approach their quarry, ears back, heads down. When the prey begins to run, the pack selects a victim and runs after that animal, chasing the antelope across the plains for up to 3 miles (5 km). In 75 percent of these chases, the dogs make a kill. Their strategy relies on speed and a kind of relay race, with dogs "cutting corners" each time the prey changes direction.

But most of Africa is thick bush and woodlands. Wild dogs in closed bush behave more like humans hunting game birds, with "beaters" flushing prey into a narrow band of open space—a road or game trail—where other members of the pack make the first attack. These chases are usually much shorter—perhaps less than half a mile, or about a kilometer—and much less successful, with perhaps only 50 percent of all attacks ending in a kill.

△ While small members of the dog family, such as foxes and jackals, are usually solitary hunters, larger canids such as the African wild dog can bring down animals as large as wildebeest by hunting in packs to exhaust their prey.

FORAGING AND STORING

Dr. Sue Healy

In an unpredictable world, animals are constantly beset with the problem of finding sufficient food—not just for survival but, more importantly, for producing as many viable offspring as they can. Some animals attempt to deal with the unpredictability of food supply by being in the right place at the right time, making calculated guesses as to where and when this might be. Those making the best calculated guesses produce more offspring.

At the other extreme are animals which, rather than give in to this unpredictability, attempt to control it. With admirable ingenuity, some animals have managed to manipulate their environment to an astonishing degree to ensure a constant supply of food.

The waiting game

One of the simplest foraging techniques is that of the filter feeders—animals that sit in one place allowing the world to wash past in the hope that the wash will contain food. Yet even this apparently simple strategy has some quite intricate adaptations which highlight the ingenuity of natural selection. Serpulid worms, for example, feed by means of a circlet of tentacles. These tentacles are covered in tiny hairs called cilia. As water is drawn through the tentacles, the cilia remove particles suspended in the water and transport them along special grooves down toward the mouth. At the mouth another set of hairs sorts the particles on the basis of size: the largest are rejected, the medium-sized particles are used to form tubes, and the smallest are eaten.

The choice of site is important for such animals. In some areas, water currents will move too slowly to provide a sufficient supply of food; in others it will move so quickly that the animal may be unable to cling to a suitable substrate.

Above: Honeybees must consume high-energy food at frequent intervals to sustain themselves and to provide enough food for the hive.
Left: Red squirrels survive through harsh winters by carefully storing several pounds of energy-rich nuts in different locations, ensuring they remain in good condition for mating and rearing young in spring.

△ Good rainfall and good weather may be a blessing to farmers, but they can also be a deadly recipe: such a combination provides a bountiful harvest of food for insect pests, encouraging locusts to breed in such numbers that they become plagues.

Fast food

Probably nowhere has the ability to process large quantities of low grade food been exploited more successfully than in the grazers and browsers. Geese, for instance, eat large amounts of food but extract very little energy from each ounce processed. The grass they eat passes through their gut very rapidly, which means that they must eat a lot in the early part of the day, until their gut is filled. They spend the rest of the day keeping their gut topped up. In the white-fronted goose, the rate at which food passes through is so great that the animal is forced to defecate every 3½ minutes—about 150 droppings in a normal feeding day.

In browsers such as grouse, food is retained in a much larger gut and for longer periods of time, thus allowing increased digestion. In addition, at the end of the small intestine some of the food passes into a special sac called a cecum for yet further digestion, while the remainder is excreted as woody droppings. The contents of the cecum are excreted separately. This enables red grouse to eat heather weighing about one tenth of its body weight per day, for its efficiency at digesting even relatively indigestible plant components such as cellulose is even greater than that of rather better known browsers like sheep and deer.

Ruminants—animals that "chew the cud"—carry this ability to break down high-fiber diets even further. Both grazing and browsing ruminants have an internal compartment in which food is fermented before it reaches the stomach, resulting in a very efficient use of protein. When the diet is poor in rapidly fermentable components and high in cellulose, food may be retained in this compartment, called a rumen, for several days.

Small but no less impressive in their ability to mow through the environment are herbivorous insects such as locusts. The appalling destruction they wreak on agricultural crops is legendary. The vast swarms may cover several hundred square miles and number as many as 300 million individuals per square mile. One advantage of moving in such large groups is the reduction in the threat that predators pose: the likelihood of any one individual being taken by a predator is minuscule. This benefit is offset, however, by the fact that because the locusts devour every piece of edible vegetation each time they alight, they are forced into traveling hundreds of miles a day to find food.

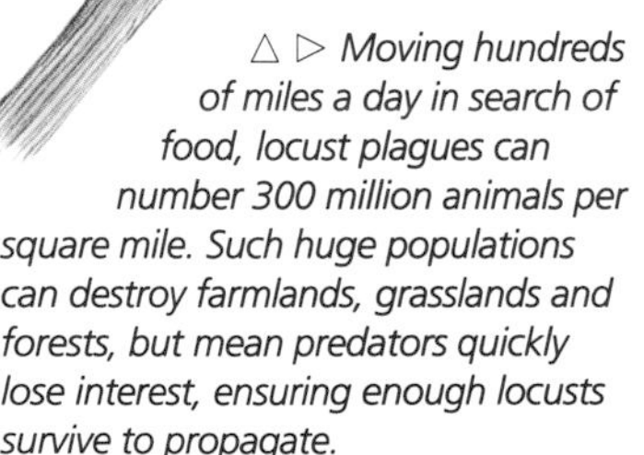

△ ▷ Moving hundreds of miles a day in search of food, locust plagues can number 300 million animals per square mile. Such huge populations can destroy farmlands, grasslands and forests, but mean predators quickly lose interest, ensuring enough locusts survive to propagate.

▷ (Opposite page) Because a female gentoo penguin must leave her chick for as many as three days while she is away hunting, she regurgitates enough semi-digested fish to keep it alive—and at the same time helps it build up the fat stores it will need to survive the chill waters of the Antarctic.

Coping with leftovers

While many food sources are not readily replenished nor suitable for territorial defense, they may occur in a quantity that provides an animal with more than one meal. When an animal finds such a large source of food, such as a flowering tree for a honeybee or a zebra carcass for a hyena, there are two options for what to do with this excess food: the animal can eat the food right away or it can hide it for eating some time later on.

While the first option seems the most obvious tactic and is also the most common, there are some costs associated with eating excess food immediately. The risk of predation may be higher because the animal, occupied with eating, remains in one place until it has finished consuming all the food. During this time it may also have to defend its feast from others of its species attempting to steal it; female lions, for example, frequently lose kills to the larger and stronger males.

One way to lower the predation risk is for the animal to decide not to attempt to eat all the food itself, and thus have the additional problem of defending the food, but to be prepared to share it. It means less food, but also less risk of being eaten, and less problem of defense.

An experimental study by Mark Elgar on sparrows at Cambridge University showed that when a slice of bread was put out, the first bird to find it proceeded quietly to eat it. When the same amount of food was crumbled, the first bird to arrive gave a "chirrup" call, which resulted in the rapid arrival of several other sparrows. In one piece the bread was defensible; crumbled it was not, and the sparrows chose to share.

Weightwatching

Another outcome of eating excess food immediately is the laying down of fat. For animals such as penguins or elephant seals the addition of fat is not just advantageous, it is crucial for insulating against the Antarctic cold. Putting on fat in preparation for migration is also highly advantageous.

For some animals, however, there are costs associated with putting on fat. This is

DEFENSE

Animals that feed on renewable food sources can provide themselves with a regular supply by defending the food source. Many nectivorous hummingbirds choose to be territorial, defending that number of flowers which will provide them with sufficient daily intake. The rufous throated hummingbird migrates from Mexico up into the Canadian Rockies and Alaska during the summer, where each bird defends a territory containing about 200 flowers of its preferred species. One technique they use to defend their flowers from raiders is to feed from the outer flowers early in the day, working their way into the center of their territories as the day proceeds. Thus they ensure that toward the end of the day the defensive effort required to see off would-be nectar thieves is small and they can spend the time acquiring sufficient nectar to get them through the night.

△ ▷ *Carnivores are opportunistic feeders, able to eat enough in one sitting to last for several days' hunting. A leopard protects its food supply from scavengers and other predators (especially lions, which obtain much of their food by scaring smaller hunters away from kills) by lodging the carcass in the fork of a tree.*

particularly true for birds, where physical changes of any description are likely to have a major impact on their capacity for flight. The impact can be observed in large birds such as geese or swans straining to get off the ground on take-off: increased size is an impediment to powered flight. Other large birds such as birds of prey and albatrosses solve the problem of getting their big bodies into the air not by increasing forward speed but by possessing wings which enable effortless gliding and by living in areas where the air currents provide sufficient lift. Nesting on cliff tops, for example, allows these birds to open their wings and literally step off the edge.

Garden raiders

There are severe limits to how much reserve food many small birds and other animals can store as fat. So they store it in a different way: by hoarding.

Some of the best known storing species are chipmunks and squirrels, perhaps because of the ease with which we can observe their storing behavior: squirrels have become infamous for their ingenuity in working out how to raid bird feeders in gardens. The same animal then often digs holes in the lawn, where it buries the raided seeds and nuts. Squirrels usually store large numbers of items in a few sites. Chipmunks store their nuts and seeds in special chambers close to their burrows, within easy reach for the periodic short intervals when they wake to feed during winter hibernation. The food stores are their sole source of energy during this period, so it is perhaps not surprising that these storage chambers may contain as many as 500 nuts.

Portable pantries

A number of storing species have developed either physical or behavioral specializations to deal with carrying away large amounts of food. A variety of vertebrates have gone in for some sort of distensible cheek pouch system, inconspicuous when empty but when fully distended able to contain an astonishing number of nuts or seeds. In rodents these cheek pouches are paired cavities opening at the angle of the lips, varying in complexity from the simple pouches of hamsters and chipmunks to the fur-lined structures of kangaroo rats and pocket mice. The capacity of these pouches varies with body size, but the energy value of the food also explains the variation in pouch size—plant-eating species have larger cheek pouches than comparably-sized grain-eating species.

Granaries for times of famine

Some of the most impressive animal larders and granaries are found in dry or semi-desert habitats, where seasonal rainfall provides a brief rich harvest. The hay or grain may be stored for the rest of the year—marked by drought—with minimal risk of fungal decay or seed germination. The granaries of the North American desert ant are so extensive that colonies are reported to have survived a severe drought which resulted in no seed crop for 12 years.

A number of species of desert rodents also store seeds in granaries inside their burrow complex. The banner-tailed kangaroo-rat has a large granary to last it the winter. Kangaroo-rats use the moisture content of the seeds as a source of water, and can control their water content by moving them from one chamber to another. But they have to strike a delicate balance between having seeds that are too dry, or so moist that they become moldy.

Sowing seeds

What of the plants whose seeds are removed by storing animal species? It seems as if the sophisticated tricks of the food storers have in turn set up selection pressures in the plants they exploit, and on which they depend. Acorns of the white oak begin to germinate very soon after being buried in the fall, apparently in an attempt to reduce the number of seeds taken and eaten by food storers. A fleshy root structure is produced, and when the storer later returns to collect the acorn, in the winter or in early spring, the connection between the acorn and the new root structure is easily broken. The new plant part, called a propagule, is left relatively unharmed and can grow into a new plant.

Yet the intrigue runs deeper still. This evasive strategy of the white oak has been countered by the gray squirrel which, in order to prevent loss of food to the potential propagule, removes the embryo from the acorn before storing it!

Rather than dissuade animals from taking their seeds, however, some plants seem positively to encourage it. Why is this? Most plants produce large numbers of small seeds in the hope that at least a few will find an appropriate place to germinate. It is even better if the parent plant can disperse its seeds, as this lowers the likelihood of competition with its offspring for local resources. Such a possibility is provided by the animal scatter hoarder: seeds are stored singly, often buried in damp soil which is ideal for germination, and, best of all, if the storer takes a large number of seeds it is likely, on occasion, to forget where it has hidden some of them. Plants that encourage storers to remove their seeds, such as beeches, produce large seeds with thin shells—a plentiful and readily accessible source of food.

△▽ Nut-, seed-, and grain-eating animals not only store food in caches, but have anatomical adaptations that help them carry food from harvest to storage. Chipmunks (above) and hamsters (below) have simple muscular pouches in their cheeks, while some rodents such as the pocket gopher have cheek pouches that open to the outside, enabling them to carry spare food and eat at the same time.

△ *Piñon jays hoard their food, carrying several seeds at a time, in scattered stores that are occasionally camouflaged to reduce pilfering. Many social species guard their caches, scaring away potential thieves.*

▽ *Many food hoarders, such as this kangaroo rat, use their sense of smell to locate their own caches, possibly following their own scent; however, these same hoarders also raid stores laid down by other members of the same species, and scavengers such as foxes and coyotes also use smell to find food stores.*

Protecting against thieves

Because they store all their food in one place, which is usually in the middle of their territory or at their nest, storers such as chipmunks and squirrels have no problem finding their caches once food becomes scarce, but they do face another problem. Because each store is a rich, highly conspicuous food source, it is a target ripe for pilferers. Some larder hoarders such as red-headed woodpeckers and eastern chipmunks will chase away any potential raider who comes too close to the storage site. Acorn woodpeckers store food communally and thus have many individuals on hand to defend their prodigious granaries.

It might seem sensible for potential pilferers simply to follow storing animals as they store food, then remove it once the storer is gone. To minimize this problem, storers are very loathe to store food in the presence of others, particularly members of their own species. But if their fellows are busy with food themselves, the storer will readily store.

By scatter-hoarding their stores, birds such as piñon jays and marsh tits are able to reduce the problem of hoard defense. Piñon jays carry several seeds at a time to each cache site, and marsh tits are even more extreme scatter-hoarders: they hide each item singly, pushing seeds deep into crevices in tree bark or under pieces of lichen. These caches are extremely well hidden, reducing the likelihood that pilferers will locate them.

Finding caches by smell

But, in making life hard for the pilferers, scatter-hoarders have in a sense made it hard for themselves as well. Piñon jays and marsh tits have no problem with cache defense, but are faced with a new problem—that of efficiently relocating their own hoards.

Experimental evidence from animals such as deer mice, kangaroo rats, red squirrels, and red foxes demonstrates the ability of these species to locate hidden food items by the sense of smell alone. Further support comes from observations of mammals sniffing in the proximity of caches then digging directly to the hidden food. Red foxes, wolves, and coyotes all scent-mark sites of caches with urine. But surprisingly, this urine marking is usually

done after the food is removed from the cache site, not as a technique for retrieval. One possible explanation is that the scent-marking informs the animal that the cached food has been removed, even though odors from the food may remain at the site.

The role of memory

Using scent cues emanating from the food itself or storing food in preferred kinds of sites still, however, leaves these hoards vulnerable to looting by other foragers. Being able to remember exactly where food has been stored will make it far less likely that the food will be systematically found by any animal other than the owner. And, formidable though the task obviously is, spatial memory for food hoards has been shown to be involved in all species where it has been investigated.

The memory of the food storing tits is remarkable. These birds store nuts and seeds singly, perhaps as many as 100 items in a day. They retrieve the food after a few hours or perhaps a couple of days; this continues throughout the year, with peaks of storing in the fall and early spring. Not only do the birds remember this large number of hidden food items, they also remember the nature and quality of the food. On retrieval trips the items they pick up first are the most preferred. For this behavior to be really advantageous, the birds should also be able to remember which sites they have removed the food from—and indeed they do avoid revisiting sites which they have emptied of food.

INGENIOUS ANIMAL LARDERS

Red squirrels hoard large numbers of seeds and nuts in a few selected places, the most conspicuous being the midden. This is a pile of cone debris found near the squirrel's nest, below the perch on which the squirrel sits to remove seeds from their cones. The debris becomes a dense mat of litter, lacking surface vegetation, in which squirrels store fresh cones. In the depths of the midden it is constantly cool and damp—an ideal place to store cones for long periods of time. But the strategy is more ingenious than this. While the cones remain damp they will not open, so the squirrel succeeds in drawing out the otherwise dangerously short season of abundance to provide itself with a long-lived supply of fresh food.

Burying acorns in damp ground may enable the squirrels to deal with another problem. Black oak acorns contain high levels of fat and thus are an excellent energy source. But they also contain high levels of tannin, which is not only unpalatable but is also thought to interfere with digestion. Depositing these acorns in damp ground provides a way of leaching out the tannins, so that when the squirrel retrieves them after several months the acorns have become quite palatable.

Maintaining food quality over time is a problem faced by all food hoarders. Those species that hoard foods like berries or animal matter are not usually able to maintain their stores for long before the food perishes, although in harsh northern winters in climes where stores usually freeze this is less of a problem. The difficulty then is thawing the food—a problem faced by owls with their well-stocked larders of frozen voles.

◁ △ *Different kinds of food hoarders employ different hoarding techniques according to their needs, their sociability, and the type of food they are storing. Mice cannot store berries underground or they will rot, so they leave several caches in tree forks (above). Acorn woodpeckers store food conspicuously, such as in the bark of trees (left), but rely on large numbers to guard caches and to scare away pilferers.*

CREATING A HOME

Dr. Michael H. Hansell

Animals that construct homes live in an artificial world of their own making. Outside, in another world, the temperature may fluctuate from scorching hot to freezing cold as night follows day, while dangerous enemies swoop and prowl. The artificial world is safe, stable—dull, even: a place to go to sleep, to rear helpless young, or, in extreme cases, to spend a whole life in.

But to create such a world an animal must be able to build. We, as builders ourselves, are impressed by the efforts of animal builders—yet some of the most impressive animal architects are relatively lowly creatures, such as insects. Impressive and ingenious houses are made even by protozoa—animals of only a single cell. An animal doesn't have to have a highly developed brain to be a builder!

Why bother to build a home?

The purpose of a home is to give the builder protection—from the dangerous fluctuations of the physical world, and from the unwelcome attentions of the biological world of predators and parasites. If the home is also portable, this portability comes at the price of speed. But as a caterpillar, for example, cannot outrun a bird anyway, carrying a home on its back is a viable option. This behavior has evolved in larvae of the moth family Psychidae, the beetle family Chrysomelidae, and the freshwater dwelling larvae of the caddis flies, where cases protect against speeding fish and sharp-jawed insect predators, and where support from the watery medium makes carrying the cases less burdensome.

But the silk produced by caddis fly larvae and caterpillars to make their homes is made of amino acids—the building blocks of protein and the essential material for animal growth. To provide themselves with protection, these animals must sacrifice

Above: Beavers select an appropriate site along a stream to build their dams, which are made of sticks, leaves, saplings and boulders, cemented together. If necessary, they will dig canals leading into the stream to float the building materials along.
Left: Many animals, such as these raccoons, find shelter in hollow tree trunks. These make an ideal ready-made home that is dry and usually safe from the majority of predators.

△ It would make sense to assume that the attraction to birds of using spider silk as a glue to aid nest building was the "sticky tape" properties of certain kinds of web. But this turns out in general not to be the case. The silk most commonly used by birds is "fluffy" spider cocoons, such as that used by the European chaffinch to hold together its mossy nest cup. So its nest is held together by the "Velcro" rather than the "Sellotape" principle. This probably has the advantage that the nest material can be continually adjusted or repaired without the silk losing its adhesive properties.

growth as well as carry the burden of the home itself. This leads to the question: does a home provide "value for money"? Is having a home more cost effective than doing without one?

For mobile or large animals already well protected by their size, the answer is no. The benefits of a home are unlikely to justify the expense. Not surprisingly, therefore, there are no home builders among horses, antelope, or deer. A wandering life and having a home don't go well together, either, so animals that spend much of their life on the move generally don't build homes. But many species that are mobile and self-sufficient as adults produce sedentary, vulnerable young. Responding to this problem has led to the evolution of a whole range of homes built purely to protect the young. The finest examples of these are built by perhaps the most obviously mobile group of all animals, the birds.

Building materials that come from the body

Like humans, animals need implements and materials to build a home. These implements are not strictly "tools," as they are almost invariably parts of the animal itself—jaws and limbs being far and away the most common. The evolution of these body parts as building implements has in fact been remarkably conservative, as they still retain their original functions of feeding and locomotion. The extraordinary range and sophistication of nests built by birds, for instance, depends almost entirely upon a sharp beak adapted more obviously for feeding than for anything else.

Sometimes, however, secretions produced by the animal's own body are used as building materials, and this has led to the evolution of specialized body features to assist construction. This is particularly well shown by animals that build with silk. It is rather extraordinary to find silken

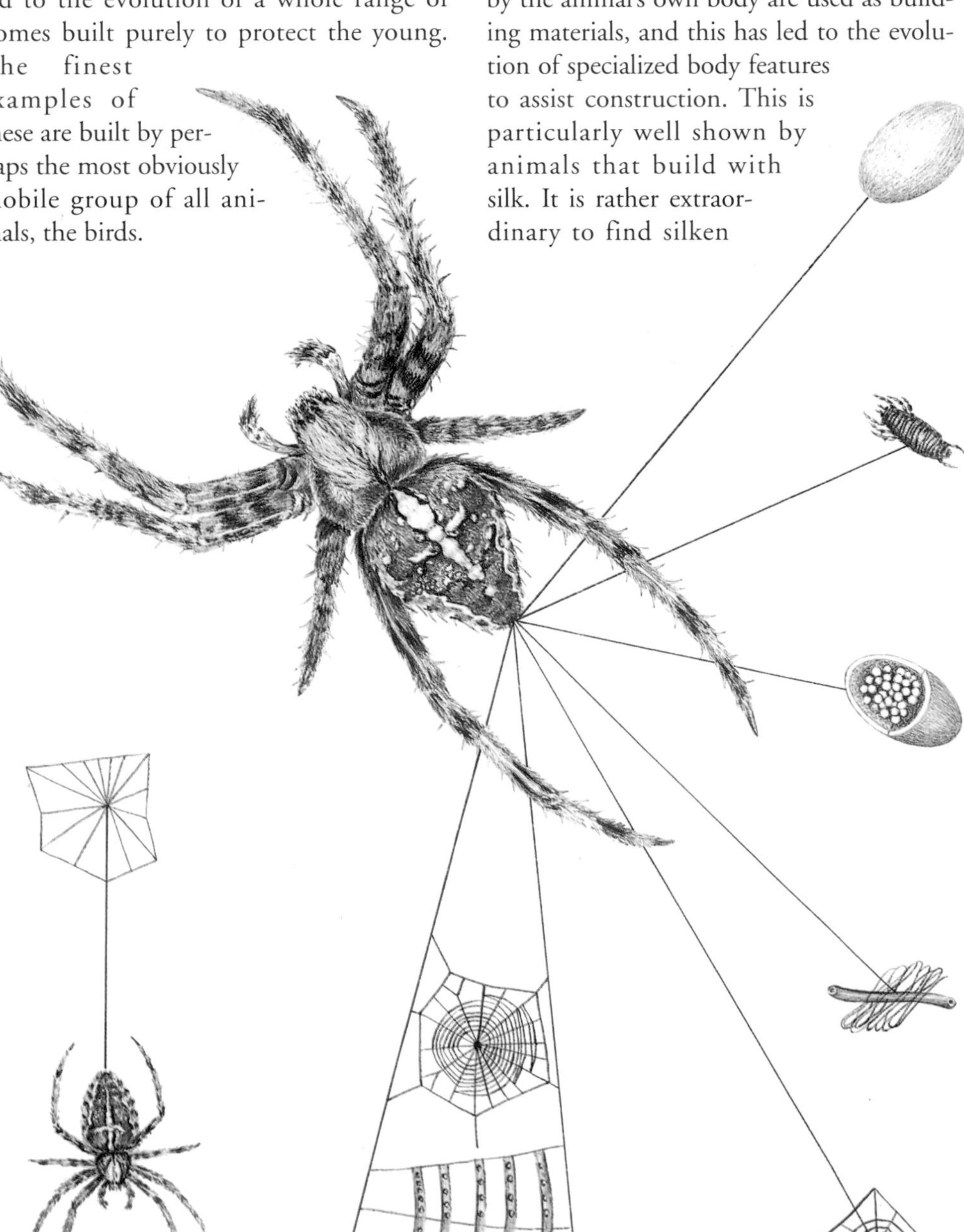

▷ The orb-web spinning garden spider has two pairs of turrets, or spinnerets, on its abdomen, each bearing numerous tiny spigots. No less than seven different kinds of glands produce two types of cocoon silk plus several kinds of web silk, all extruded through the spigots. The web silks include sticky capture silk and cement to attach the threads to one another.

threads which are biochemically very similar yet are produced by two quite distinct arthropod groups, insects and spiders. Spiders have probably the most complicated and specialized silk extrusion devices.

Another substance, mucus, which is normally secreted in the mouths of vertebrates to keep the lining moist and to lubricate it for swallowing food, has in the edible-nest swiftlet become the sole material for creating a tiny, brittle nest. This is the basis for the bland, glutinous delicacy, bird's nest soup. Another mucus-like substance probably forms the coating of the air bubbles blown by male Siamese fighting fish and related paradise fish to make floating nests in which they deposit eggs.

The fur and feathers that cover the bodies of adult mammals and birds can be pulled out and placed in the lining of the nest to perform exactly the same function in the protection of the naked young. Fecal waste is a rather less obvious self-secreted home-building material, yet it forms an important part of the home of some minute aquatic rotifers, of the defensive shield of the larvae of the cassida beetle species, and parts of the cases or pupal cocoons of some caterpillars. The fecal pellets of most caterpillars are regular in shape and contain little water, so they make ideal building bricks. The caterpillar of the hypertropha species of the Australian moth has, by evolving a method of expelling its pellets not singly but in groups of three or four that stick together to form a rod, created natural pillars with which to make the frame of a house. The caterpillar secures a rod with silk at one end to the leaf surface, with another rod close by. A third rod placed on top allows the caterpillar to lash the two pillars together with silk, forming an arch. Additional arches form a corridor when the walls are filled in with more silk.

The nomadic New World army ants possess the ultimate self-generated building material: their own bodies. Worker ants of the species link their bodies together by their claws to create a kind of living chain mail. This live nest material is actually capable of dynamic adjustment in response to changing conditions within the nest. The curtain of ant bodies is arranged to form ventilation spaces and passages, which can be opened up to increase air flow or closed down to retain heat. These changes are achieved by changes in the body positions of what may be hundreds of thousands of interlocked ants.

△ *Just as many caterpillars construct cocoons from their own silk, others utilize fecal waste—which is dry, odorless (so it does not attract predators) and regular in shape as "building bricks" with which to make a shelter, inside which they can undergo the transformation from caterpillar to moth or butterfly.*

Building materials that come from nature

Despite the importance of self-secreted building materials, the majority of building materials are collected by animals from the habitats in which they live. All can be classified as animal, vegetable, or mineral.

Birds are the best illustrators of the variety of possible animal-produced building materials. Many birds make use of the fur or feathers of other animals and birds, but the most important animal material for small tree-nesting bird species is spider silk. There are at least 20 families of such birds in which

▽ *Army ants use their own tight-packed bodies to form bivouacs, or temporary shelters, as they move in search of food. Few predators would risk the painful bites and stings of these fierce ants, which can protect the queen, eggs and larvae by adjusting their positions to form ventilation spaces or an impenetrable shield of bodies.*

△ *Bird nests range from the shallow scrape used by some seabirds to the elaborate and beautifully constructed hanging nests of weaver birds, made of tightly interwoven grass stalks. The pendant nest, usually suspended from a narrow branch, protects the eggs and nestlings from all but the lightest and most persistent predators.*

▽ *Eagles are relatively heavy birds and cannot manipulate nesting materials with their beaks or feet. They build nests simply by piling sticks in a tree fork or on a rock ledge. They make little attempt to interweave the sticks, relying instead on their own weight to pack the material into a stable mass.*

many or all of the species make use of spider silk. Whether or not this creates serious problems for spiders we have no idea.

Among the more puzzling nesting materials used by birds is snakeskin. It is a typical material in the nests of a number of species, including some New World flycatchers such as the western kingbird, Bewick's wren, and the paradise riflebird. One theory is that the snakeskin may serve to scare away would-be predators such as small mammals or other bird species.

A wide range of plant materials is used by animals in home building. Grasses and pieces of palm frond are favored by many bird species because, with their long parallel veins, they are very amenable to being intertwined. Large birds such as eagles and storks prefer twigs and sticks, while the smallest birds such as some hummingbirds make a nest cup almost entirely out of the very fine down found in some seed pods.

Minerals favored by animals amount essentially to mud, sand, and pebbles. Mud is a heavy building material, so it is surprising to find that cliff swallows can secure their mud nests to overhanging cliffs without them falling off. Barn swallows can attach their nests to the vertical walls under concrete bridges—but observers have noticed that in this situation they frequently make use of the mud nests of solitary wasps as a foundation for their own nest.

Animal building techniques

Stones, mud, and grass are not only abundant and cheap for animals to collect, they also demand the use of fairly obvious building techniques. Bricks must be piled up or stuck together, mud must be molded, and long grass strands must be woven together.

The molding principle of construction depends on the animal shaping a plastic material which then changes to the solid state needed in the completed home. But it is not usually possible for the animal to gather all the material needed for construction in one load. This creates a potential problem: the material will dry out between loads which have not fused together properly, and cracks will develop. Some mud-daubing wasps overcome this by making a buzzing noise as they spread a fresh load of mud. This temporarily liquefies the mud, allowing tiny air bubbles to escape and the new load to weld firmly onto the existing structure. Similar vibratory movements are shown by the white-winged chough as it applies mud to its nest. This apparently allows the mud to flow between the plant fibers which, together with the mud, form the compound nest material.

The African and Asian weaverbirds are best known for the craft of weaving with strands of plant material, although this craft has also been mastered by members of other bird families and even by a species of shrimp, which uses its fine claws to weave together strands of algae to form a shelter. The great advantage of weaving is that a home can be created using only one type of material. The disadvantage is that the weaving itself must be skillful enough to prevent the whole structure from falling apart. When this happens to us, our response is usually to slap on a bit of glue. Other animals also find this solution effective, and have found or produced for themselves a variety of different "glues"—such as mucus, silk, and plant resins—which are often used to stick building materials together.

THE BUSY BEAVER

△ Apart from some desert rats and mice, the beaver is the only rodent able to walk on its hind legs. It carries building material to its lodge in its mouth and supported on its front limbs, then it packs it in place with its powerful tail.

For all its remarkable ability to construct massive lodges and dams, the beaver has no features of its anatomy entirely specialized for that role. It does have highly developed, continuously growing incisor teeth which enable it to fell substantial trees, but this wood is used not just to build lodges or dams but also to supply bark, the winter diet of beavers. The front unwebbed feet have large claws for digging but are not otherwise notably specialized.

Perhaps the most surprising attribute of the beaver is its ability to walk on its hind legs. This enables it to carry building materials such as twigs, and also offspring, cradled between the upper surface of the "arms" and the chin.

△ If the lodge is damaged by water or by a large predator such as a bear, the female beaver will pick up her young, called kits, and carry them to a safe place while the lodge is repaired.

▽ As winter approaches, adult beavers collect leaves, twigs and shoots, swimming with a bundle of twigs held behind their massive top incisors then carrying the load of winter food into the lodge, where it remains fresh and palatable for many weeks.

A completely different home making technique involves not putting together but taking away: that is burrowing. Many animals dig into the ground, or into riverbanks or cliff faces, to create tunnels and/or chambers for use as a home, from tiny lobster-like marine creatures to mammals such as foxes, moles, wombats, and badgers. The subterranean Callianassa looks rather like a small (about 1½ inch, or 3–4 cm) skinny lobster, but it does not hide away under rocks for shelter. Instead, it digs itself a vertical shaft some 12–30 inches (30–80 cm) deep, straight down into the fine mud of the sea bed. At the bottom of this shaft it constructs a complex system of branching tunnels, swollen in places to provide ten or so chambers. The purpose of these chambers is still unclear, but one suggestion is that they are gardens from the walls of which Callianassa harvests micro-organisms.

◁ The fennec, a small fox in the deserts of North Africa, excavates a deep, cave-like burrow, occupied by up to ten individuals, in hard-packed sand dunes or cliff faces. Fennecs have also been known to take over disused burrows abandoned by larger foxes or aardvarks.

△ *Chimpanzees, our closest living relatives, are home builders—but their efforts are unimpressive not only by our own standards but by those of birds, wasps, and even many a caterpillar. The "home" a chimp builds is in fact nothing more than a bed for the night. In the morning it moves on, leaving its nest behind. The next evening it will build another nest in another tree, breaking tree branches inwards across each other and intertwining them a little for strength. The whole process takes no more than a few minutes.*

A home is a castle

In the most highly developed examples of the home as a defensive structure—the nests built by leaf-cutter ants and the mounds built by termites—the home becomes a fortress shielding sometimes millions of colony members from a hostile world into which many of them never even venture. In termites of the Nasutitermes species, for example, journeys from the nest located high up in a tree to the ground where plant food is collected are undertaken entirely through a system of covered highways roofed with plant fragments and fecal cement.

Some animals provide themselves with extra protection by building their home inside the homes of other species. About 50 species of birds, notably kingfishers and parrots, build their nests in the regulated environment of termite mounds. Some tropical social bees and wasps build their nests inside those of pugnacious ant species. To prevent being attacked by the ants, one wasp smears the outside of its nest with a waxy secretion that smells like the ants.

Pests—and pesticides

The other side of this coin, of course, is when your own home offers the prospect of free accommodation—and food—to other species, particularly parasites that enter by stealth and destroy from within. Birds with fleas and lice, for example, risk passing them on to their chicks. These parasites can multiply enormously in the protected environment of the nest, with a food supply that cannot escape. One hundred thousand blood-sucking mites have been found in the nest hole of a European starling. Flea populations can even overwinter in the nest and attack the brood the following spring.

Some birds do, however, seem to have a means of combating this threat: they bring fresh plant material with insecticidal properties to the nest. Species demonstrating this behavior include Harris's hawk and the bald eagle, as well as tree-hole nesters like the European starling. One herb used by the starling is Erigeron, known to us as fleabane (the flea killer).

The Eastern screech owl of North America seems to have devised a unique method of controlling nest cavity parasites. The owl's prey is normally brought to the nest already killed, but blind snakes are carried back alive. It seems that the blind snake keeps the parasite population down: in nests containing live blind snakes, chicks have been found to grow faster and have a better chance of survival.

▷ *The homes of some bagworms are particularly well-designed cases, made to resist attacks from the beaks of birds. The bagworms cut straight lengths of stick in the manner of a beaver gnawing through a tree. In one instance these are laid parallel to the case axis to make a cylindrical wall; in another, more sophisticated design they are laid across the case axis to form a three-sided wall that twists spirally along the case so that the case is hard to crush from whatever angle a bird attacks. This elaborate design is costly in terms of construction effort, but the effectiveness makes it worthwhile.*

BASKET-WEAVING BIRDS

△ ▷ *Weaverbirds use such a variety of techniques to build their complex nests that humans have adopted some of their interlocking loops, hitches and knots in making cane containers*

The true weaverbirds belong to the *Ploceinae* family, a subfamily of the sparrow family. Their technological breakthrough seems to have been a change from dry to fresh green strips of grass and palm leaf, which are highly flexible and tough. "Weaving" is in fact rather a misleading term for their complex construction techniques, which include spiral and alternately reversed winding, interlocking loops, hitches, and knots. The nest of the weaverbird *Malimbus cassini*, for example, has a particularly long entrance tube, ingeniously woven so that the strands of the weave spiral down in contrary directions. A snake trying to get to the nest entrance finds it hard to maintain a purchase on the tube which, because of its design, shrinks within its grasp. The nests are hung from a fine branch, often over water.

Although they deserve their high reputation as builders, the weaverbirds are by no means the only group of birds that build and hang a nest using only long strands of vegetation. This technique is also used by a member of the babbler family in New Guinea, and in the New World by oropendolas and caciques. A small and handsome member of the starling family, the metallic starling, designs and builds a hanging basket using mainly interlocking vine tendrils.

◁ *The leafcutter ants of South America cultivate their own food by growing special fungus gardens. The ants leave the nest to collect vegetation. Leaf fragments are chewed into small pieces, mixed with saliva, fertilized with excrement, then inserted into the huge sponge-like mounds of fungus. The fungus, in turn, breaks down the cellulose of the leaves into digestible food for the ants. So the fungus feeds on the leaves; the ants feed on the fungus. It has been estimated that to keep the huge nests supplied with fresh plant material, in some forests leafcutter ants may consume over 15 percent of all leaf production.*

Termite Mounds

Dr. D. M. Gordon

△ *The mounds built by the so-called magnetic termites of northern Australia are aligned precisely from north to south to take advantage of temperature differences of the eastern and western sides of the mound to enable the interior to be kept at a regulated temperature.*

Many species of animals make communal dwellings, where large families, or groups of families, live together in a single home. The social insects—ants, bees, wasps, and termites—build homes that are amazing in their size, complexity, and variety. By living together, animals can work together. When an animal lives alone, or with its mate and offspring, a few animals must accomplish many tasks: find food, build and repair the nest, and take care of the young. When large groups live together, the same tasks can be divided up among many animals. This may be why communal living is widespread among many different kinds of animals, including birds and mammals as well as insects.

The Sears Tower in Chicago is, at 1454 feet (443 m), the tallest building in the world. It's the height of about 250 people standing on one another's heads. But the highest termite mounds, at 20 feet (6 m), are taller than about 1000 termite workers laid end to end. In fact, in proportion to their size, termites build the largest structures of all living creatures.

Termites are social insects that eat cellulose, a component of many plants. Some species nest in wood and feed on the wood in which they live; the dry wood termites simply live in galleries in the wood as they feed upon it. Other termites nest in soil and go out of the nest to collect wood, vegetation, and seeds which they bring back to the nest to feed upon.

Termite nests are often begun after a mating flight, when thousands of winged reproductive forms pour out of many neighboring nests. One male and one female will found a new nest together near a rock or piece of wood. At first the pair lives in a tiny chamber, about a half inch (1 cm) wide, just an inch or so (about 2 cm) below the surface of the soil. The following spring, the first worker offspring emerge and construct a larger nest, with many galleries.

◁ *Other species of termites build massive, fortress-like mounds designed to withstand the infrequent flooding rains of arid Australia. These mounds rely on a complex system of tunnels and chambers to funnel air to the interior; worker termites also moisten the walls of the chambers to cool the air by means of evaporation.*

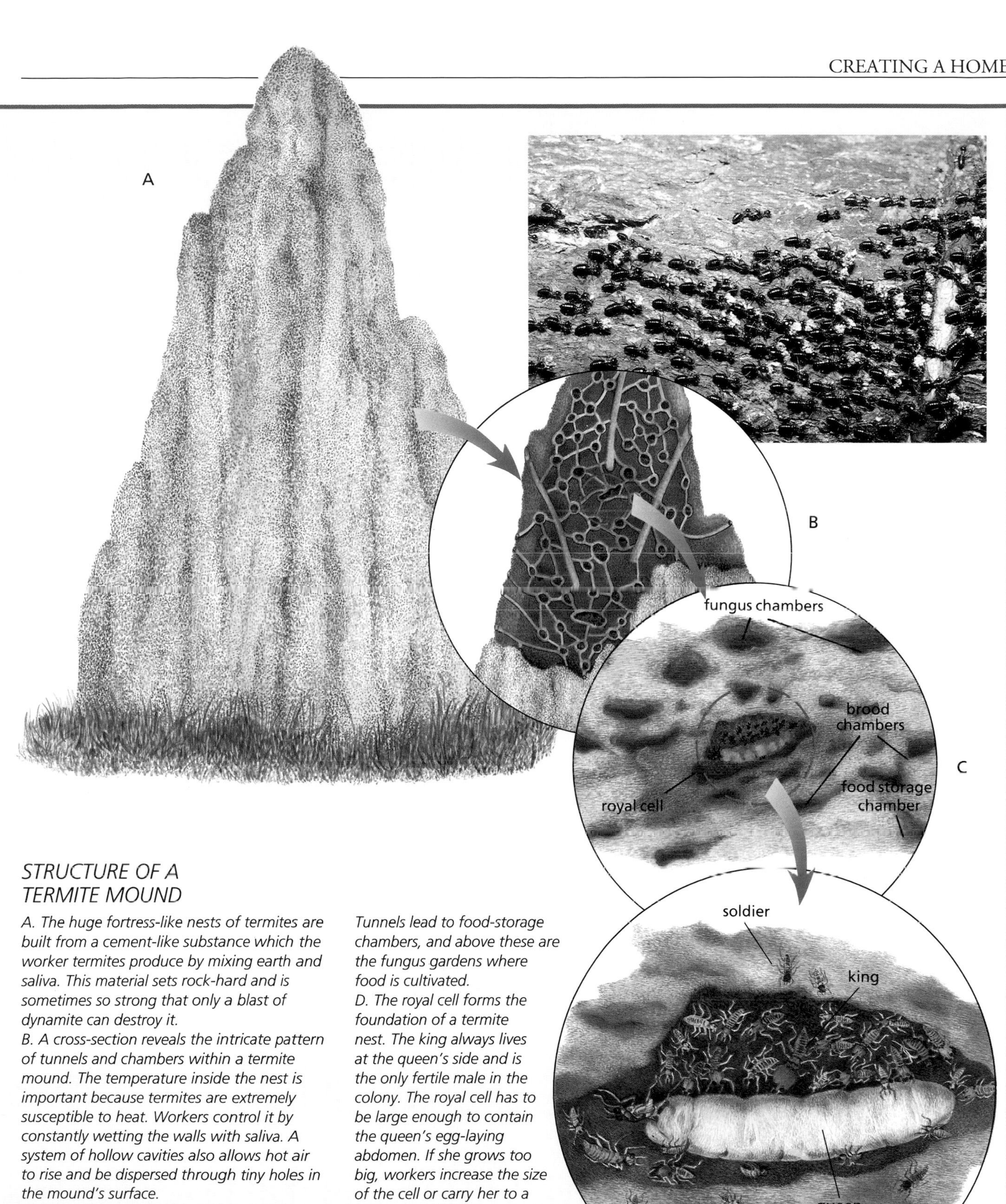

STRUCTURE OF A TERMITE MOUND

A. The huge fortress-like nests of termites are built from a cement-like substance which the worker termites produce by mixing earth and saliva. This material sets rock-hard and is sometimes so strong that only a blast of dynamite can destroy it.

B. A cross-section reveals the intricate pattern of tunnels and chambers within a termite mound. The temperature inside the nest is important because termites are extremely susceptible to heat. Workers control it by constantly wetting the walls with saliva. A system of hollow cavities also allows hot air to rise and be dispersed through tiny holes in the mound's surface.

C. Around the royal cell in which the king and queen live and breed are the brood chambers where the eggs are taken after hatching. Tunnels lead to food-storage chambers, and above these are the fungus gardens where food is cultivated.

D. The royal cell forms the foundation of a termite nest. The king always lives at the queen's side and is the only fertile male in the colony. The royal cell has to be large enough to contain the queen's egg-laying abdomen. If she grows too big, workers increase the size of the cell or carry her to a larger chamber.

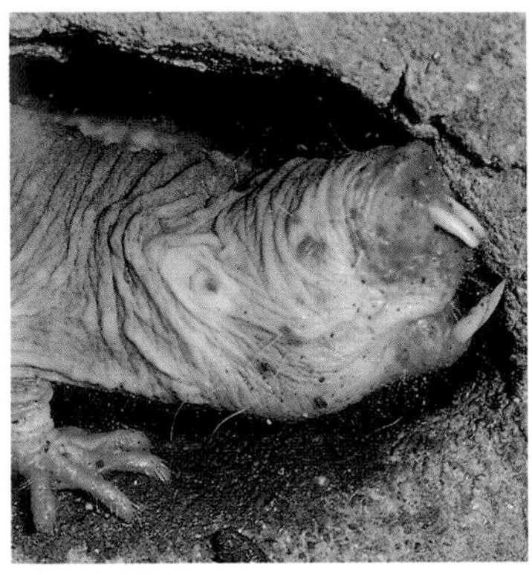

△ The naked mole-rat of eastern Africa lives in large, related groups in which only the dominant female reproduces. With hundreds of individuals occupying the same complex, the system of burrows and chambers that develops can extend for more than 300 feet, including many layers of tunnels.

▽ The sett, or burrow, of the European badger may contain several chambers used by individual badgers for nesting or rearing young. Despite their communal lifestyle, badgers do not co-operate in excavating the sett or in taking care of the young, but appear to take advantage of the convenience of an existing home, which individuals enlarge to suit their own needs.

Fixtures and fittings

A bird's nest may at first sight appear to be just a cup, or a mouse burrow just a hole, but many animal homes have various special features inside the protective outer layer. The nest cup of a bird may be lined with soft feathers to prevent damage to the eggs and insulate them against heat loss. The burrow of a woodmouse contains a bedchamber with nesting materials, other chambers where food may be stored, and two or more entrance burrows to make coming and going less risky. Many species build special larders for food storage (see the chapter Foraging and Storing).

Making a home encourages social life

The shy, modest European badger lives in elaborate burrow systems (setts) in groups of three to 10 individuals, yet in many respects badgers don't seem to be very social. They don't cooperate in the care of their young; when sleeping in the sett they avoid one another's company; they hunt alone and show no group defense. So why do they live together at all?

One interesting possibility is that it is the burrow system that creates the society. Badgers tend to stay in their home sett because of the cost of making a new one. As a result, setts get gradually larger and more elaborate. Some badger setts grow to immense size. One sett, partially excavated because of a road widening project, was found to consist of over half a mile (nearly a kilometer) of branching tunnels, 50 nest chambers, and 178 exits. We have no idea how long a sett like this has been in existence, but it may not be fanciful to suggest that it is hundreds of years. There are at least 25 village names in England containing the word "badger" or "brock," including Badgers Mount and Brockholes, suggesting that long-term occupation by badgers gave each village its name.

Naked mole rats

The naked mole rat is a funny-looking rodent that lives in large social groups, in which only one female reproduces at a time. All the others help in the construction of the nest, foraging, and care of the young. The burrow systems of mole-rats may extend for more than 300 feet (100 m), including many layers of tunnels. New tunnels are constructed after rains, when the soil is softer and easier to dig.

The burrow system is elaborate. There is a set of superficial burrows, each one only just over an inch (about 3 cm) in diameter, just wide enough for one mole rat to pass through. Leading down from the superficial burrows are connecting burrows, which go to the highway burrows. Mole rats eat roots, tubers, and bulbs, which they find underground; the highway burrows serve as the roads from the nest to the foraging area. These highways are always more than 20 inches (50 cm) underground, and they are about 2 inches (4–5 cm) wide, enough for two mole rats to pass each other. At T–junctions, however, they may have to make a 3–point turn. Some of the highway burrows contain blind-end tunnels that are used for passing. Below the highway burrows are the nest chambers, which contain stored food and the youngest animals. Nest chambers sometimes have bolt holes, blind-ended tunnels that descend very steeply, which may be used as a place to escape during an emergency.

ANTS' NESTS

Dr. D. M. Gordon

Different species of ants make an enormous variety of nests. Ants with small colonies construct tiny nests in hollow acorns or twigs. At the other extreme are species with huge colonies, such as the fungus-growing ants in Central America, with nests that extend for hundreds of yards and may be up to 20 feet (6 m) deep. Nests of these species have been found with a thousand entrances at the surface, and a thousand chambers inside.

Weaver ants construct nests out of silk spun by the larvae. This silk binds the leaves of a tree together to form a protected cavity. When workers extend their nest, they begin by building a link between the edges of two leaves. They do this by forming a chain; one ant holds onto the next with its jaws, or mandibles. Workers form rows of these chains to hold the leaves together. Then other workers carry larvae from inside the existing nests. A worker holds onto a larva, and touches its head to each of the two connecting points at leaf edges. In between these two points, the larva spins a strand of silk. In this way, a whole wall of silk is formed.

Many ant species nest in the soil. For example, the seed-eating ants of the southwestern United States construct tunnels about 7 feet (2 m) deep. This is impressive, because the soil of the desert can be leached hard as rock. After the summer mating flight, a new colony is founded by a newly mated queen. She digs a hole an inch or two (a few centimeters) below the surface, then extends this into a tunnel. The following spring, the first workers emerge to forage. Within a few years, the colony will contain thousands of workers and a complex gallery of chambers.

The ants pack the sides of the chambers with wet soil which dries into a hard surface like adobe. The chambers have curved roofs and flat bottoms. Some hold stored seeds, the colony's food supply; others hold brood. The queen spends most of her time at the bottom of the nest but sometimes, during the heat of the day, the workers bring the brood up to the chambers just underneath the surface. When the larvae and pupae are warm, they grow faster. So by moving the brood around the nest, the ants can regulate how fast the larvae and pupae grow into adult workers.

All of the world's many thousands of species of ants are communal insects, building nests that range from the temporary shelters composed of the bodies of the ants themselves, such as the driver ants of Central and South America (left) to the nests built of stitched-together leaves by African weaver ants (above) and Australian green ants (below.)

BEE COLONIES

Dr. D. M. Gordon

△ *Some species of bees are solitary or live in small groups that lack differentiated "castes" of queen, drones, workers, and so on.*

▷ *Most bee colonies are enormous, consisting of up to 100,000 or more individuals, each with a strictly defined role. The European honeybee has evolved a colony structure that includes specialized castes, responsible for collecting food and care of the eggs, larvae, and pupae.*

Many of the thousands of species of bees live in communal dwellings. The size of a bee colony may be tiny, only one bee and her larvae, or enormous, as in tropical stingless honeybees, with up to 180,000 bees. The nest of a bee colony is where eggs are laid, where the brood (eggs, then larvae, then pupae or cocoons) are cared for, and where adults spend their time when they are not out foraging. The smallest nest is a burrow, consisting of only a small tunnel in the ground. Species with larger colonies, such as honeybees, have nests that occupy a cavity in a tree or between rocks. Inside the cavity the bees build an elaborate structure of cells.

In the sweat bees, each bee works at nest construction as well as going out to forage. Several bees work together to construct a new cell, in which the queen will lay an egg, and to bring pollen into the cell as food for the larva that hatches. In the bumblebees, new cells for newly-laid eggs are constructed on top of clumps of cocoons. Each egg passes through a larval stage, then becomes a cocoon, and eventually hatches out as an adult. The growing larvae are fed by the newly-hatched adults. The number of new cells made depends on the number of cells occupied by cocoons. As the growing larvae will be fed by their older sisters, this system may ensure that each newly-laid egg will have enough older bees to care for it.

In highly social bees such as stingless honeybees, the nest, inside a hollow tree, has a complex architecture with recognizably different parts. There are stacks of combs of hexagonal cells for rearing the brood, and, in a separate area, globular storage pots for holding honey and pollen. Surrounding the combs is a collection of sinuous branching pillars.

The cells for eggs, the storage cells for food, and the pillars are made of cerumen, a wax-like material consisting of wax secreted by the bees plus plant resin. Bees secrete cerumen from their own wax-making body cells, but they also recycle it from empty storage pots, from old brood cells, and from a special rubbish heap where old cerumen is dumped when it is no longer needed. When the larvae inside brood cells begin to form cocoons, the cerumen walls of the brood cells are no longer needed, and workers begin to thin them down, taking the wax to build new brood cells. Bees cut off strips of wax from the heap of discarded cerumen and, using their mandibles, apply these strips to the walls of a new cell.

A new colony of honeybees is formed from an old one when there is a swarm, containing a new queen, males, and some workers. The swarm chooses a cavity in which to make its new nest. The workers use plant gums, called propolis, to seal off all the cracks and openings in the cavity except for one entrance hole; this helps to hold in heat and moisture.

Inside the cavity, the colony constructs layers of combs. The first comb is begun on the top or side of the new nest cavity. Many bees work together on comb construction, each bee apparently working independently. Any individual will do many of the tasks that produce combs: add wax, smooth it, or cut it away. As the comb grows, wax is added to the lower edge by some bees. The irregular clumps of wax are formed into round cells, and each new cell is inserted in the angle between two existing cells. The bees don't appear to communicate with each other, and there is no bee directing the work of others. But somehow, the result of all the bees' individual decisions is a perfect array of hexagonal cells.

Cells in the combs of honeybees are used to store pollen and nectar, and the eggs, larvae, and pupae of immature bees. It seems that honeybees are stimulated to produce wax when there is a surplus of nectar collected by foraging bees: when there is not enough room for all the nectar being collected, some bees store the nectar inside their digestive tract. Bees that hold a surplus of nectar then begin to secrete wax.

Different sized cells are used for male bees, worker bees, and for the bees that will become reproductive females, or queens. Whether a female becomes a sterile worker or a reproductive queen depends on how much she is fed as a larva. In turn, how much she is fed seems to be determined by the cell in which she was laid. In some way, the sizes and shapes of cells determine how many males, workers, and new queens the colony will produce.

▽ (Left) Many members of the colony are engaged in building and maintaining the hive, each working independently to produce wax and to build or repair cells. Such is the power of instinct that thousands of bees making individual decisions construct a perfect array of hexagonal cells that makes the optimum use of available space.

▽ In tropical climates or where the colony is protected from inclement weather or sudden changes in temperature, the hive is sometimes constructed in the open. In these situations, repair and maintenance to the exterior of the hive occupy much of the lives of large numbers of workers.

THE SOCIAL ANIMAL

COMMUNICATING

Dr. David Robinson

Although animals don't have language in the way we understand it, their communication systems are often sophisticated and highly refined. They can communicate in a number of different ways: via vibration, exemplified by deathwatch beetles; electricity, such as in electric fish; touch, as in honeybees; light (reflected, as in chimpanzees, and generated, as in fireflies); sound, as in crickets; gesture, as in monkeys; and chemical secretion, as in moths. No single animal, however, exploits all the available methods.

Animals use their various communication systems to signal information to each other.

We humans can detect and appreciate some of the methods of communication animals use, such as the beautiful warning colors of certain moths, but we can't hear most bat signals and we can't smell female moths signaling to males. We cannot, in fact, detect or understand the full range of animal communication systems without scientific help, as many signals contain information in coded form.

Coded and uncoded messages

All animal signals contain information, but the signal often will not be directly associated with the information. The meerkat does not try to imitate a hawk when warning its burrow-mates of the approach of a predatory hawk. It uses a short signal that is the code for a hawk. Most animal signals carry information in a coded form which the recipient has to decode, so for communication within related animals it is reasonable to expect that the recipient knows the code.

Signals that are intended for a range of different animals, such as the warning flash of a pair of eye spots, may be uncoded. The message here is unambiguous: eye spots threaten! Many small fish and insects pretend to be large and threatening by displaying eye spots to predators.

While animal language is unlike human language, both consist of codes that communicate information about the individual and the world. Animal languages employ signals rather than words, from the Central American bullseye silk moth's eye-spots (above), used to startle would-be attackers, to the postures and repertoire of chattering, whining and barking noises used by the African meerkat (left) to warn companions of predators.

Communicating identity

Species identity is important in bringing individuals of the same species together for mating; identity signals may also serve to allow members of an established pair to recognize each other subsequently. And the sounds produced by some whales are so distinctive that it is at least possible that any one individual "knows" all the other members of the species in the world by their sounds.

Parents and offspring may need to identify each other by signals. The common tern, for instance, fishes offshore and then returns to the colony to feed the young. As the parent flies in it gives a characteristic call that its own chicks recognize. They reply with their call, and so the parent manages to locate them in the densely populated colony.

Signals can also indicate membership of a social group. In social insects such as honeybees, the colony has a unique chemical signal of its own. Interlopers can be recognized by their unfamiliar odor, and thus either prevented from entering the hive or killed.

▽ The eerie and beautiful "songs" produced by humpback whales are based on themes common to all members of the local population. Each extended population sings the same song, with minor variations (which may serve to identify smaller groups) that is so distinctive that even scientists can tell where a particular whale comes from by its song.

Signaling sexual availability

Adult animals are not always ready to mate. Male crickets and newts, for example, have a cycle of receptivity governed by sperm depletion, while female primates are usually only receptive at one stage of the estrus cycle. This stage is signaled in some species by a reddening and swelling of the skin around the vagina. In crickets the signal is acoustic: the males sing to attract a female. The song carries the message "I am sexually motivated" as well as identity information. It is possible that the signal also gives information about the quality of the male. In some species of cricket, females are known to choose the loudest song, and the loudest singer may be the largest or the closest male.

Mating calls have information encoded in them about the identity and reproductive status of the caller, and their physical properties give additional information about where the caller is located. The signal acts as a homing beacon. Provided that the receiving animal can scan the environment to find the direction in which the signal is strongest, it can track down the caller.

Environmental influences

Some means of communication are available only in certain environments. For instance, in the deep sea there is no light, so animals communicating visually must either generate their own light or exploit other communication channels. And once signals are broadcast they are degraded by the environment. Most visual signals depend on reflected daylight, so are less effective in low light conditions and useless

A Long-range Beacon

The female silk moth releases a scent, called bombykol, from a gland on her abdomen. The scent is highly attractive to the male silk moth—indeed, it is one of the most effective beacons in the insect world. The male has feathery antennae covered with receptors which can respond to single molecules of the female's scent. This extraordinary sensitivity means that the female can attract a male who is nearly a mile away. All the male has to do is to fly into the wind and track the plume of scent being carried toward him. Initially, the male is able to fly only in the general direction of the female. But as he gets closer, the scent gets stronger and he can fly up a "scent gradient" that leads him directly to his mate. The receptors on the antennae of the male are not only very sensitive but also very selective. Synthetic bombykol, which is chemically identical to the natural scent, will attract a male, but if a synthetic molecule of a slightly different shape is used it will be substantially less attractive to the male. The antennae of the female are much smaller and, not surprisingly, are not specialized for detecting bombykol. They are probably specialized for detecting the characteristic odors from suitable sites to lay her eggs.

△ *Male silk moths find a mate using a language based on a chemical message. Female moths emit airborne messages based on sex hormones called pheromones. The males have such sophisticated antennae that the scents can be detected at distances of up to a mile, and followed along a "scent gradient" of increasing concentration.*

◁ *Red deer males, or stags, proclaim their territories by roaring, emitting loud bellows that echo around the hills and warn competing males to stay away. Often, however, a stag's roaring encourages rivals to enter a sound contest that may signal attractive qualities such as fitness, strength and endurance to females.*

at night. Chemical signals are directional when released, as the molecules are dispersed by air currents, but the animal emitting the scent has no control over which way the signal goes, nor what other scents it is competing against. Sounds get weaker as they travel through the air, eventually becoming inaudible. For long-range communication, low pitched sounds are better as they remain audible over a longer distance than high pitched sounds. Sound signals may also be swamped by other sounds.

Body language

Much can be communicated by, for example, facial expression in monkeys or body posture in birds. The male green heron responds initially to both males and females approaching the nest by standing with his head thrust forward and his feathers erect. This indicates that he is ready to lunge at the intruder with his bill, which is pointed and dangerous. If the female persists, instead of being rebuffed, the behavior of the male changes, indicating that he is prepared to consider her advances. The

Sirens of the Insect World

Fireflies are beetles that are able to emit light as short intense flashes. The light is a yellow-green color in most species, although blue-white, white, and red lights are known. This light signal acts as a beacon to bring the sexes together for mating, but it also carries information encoded in the flashes. The flashes are very brief, usually a fraction of a second in duration. Males produce trains of flashes in which the number, color, and timing of the flashes denotes the species he belongs to. If a female recognizes the pattern she will respond with a flash, or pattern of flashes, that is likewise species-specific. The timing of her reply is linked to the male's flashes. As soon as the male sees her response he flies down and they mate. In fact, the sky may be full of males looking for a female's answering flash, so there can be intense competition. There is a premium on a fast response by the male. But this fast response has been exploited by other species. Fireflies are predators, and the females of some species produce a bogus reply to a male of another species and then consume him when he arrives. Some females are known to have a repertoire of four or five different flash sequences that mimic other species and attract males of those species to their doom. However, males of one species are known to be able to detect the false signal before getting close enough to the female to be attacked.

There is a further level of complexity in this battle between predators and prey. There are males of a predatory species that mimic the flash pattern of a prey species. This stimulates females of the same species as the males to reply in the expectation of finding supper, using the appropriate mimic signal. Having located the female, the male lands and switches to his own signal, thus mating with the female but, presumably, leaving her hungry.

▽ ▷ The winking flashes of light produced by fireflies contain codes that specify these predatory beetles' sex and species. Females of some species exploit the eagerness to mate of males from their species by emitting a bogus reply that lures the male to his death.

threatening bill is lowered and the feathers lowered. Then the male stretches upward, gently swaying. This posture is very different from the earlier, threatening display and gives the female a clear signal that instead of being rebuffed she will be permitted to enter the nest.

In monkey and ape societies, facial expressions can convey a wealth of information. When an adult male baboon yawns, exposing the large canine teeth, it is a threat. So effective is it that a yawn of a dominant male will divert a subordinate male and no damaging fight will take place. The facial expressions of chimps are so close to our own that we get the same message as a chimp. The begging chimp looking at a feeding adult has an expression that is instantly recognizable. If the longing glance proves unsuccessful, the begging chimp can follow it up with an open palm.

◁ *An adult male baboon makes a threatening display, exposing his large canine teeth.*

Electric fish

Electric fish communicate by pulses of electricity conducted through the water. There are two sorts of electric fish: those that produce electrical pulses to stun prey or deter predators, and those that produce relatively weak electrical signals used for communication. These latter fish are found in fresh water in both Africa and South America.

The signals are a series of pulses ranging from 10 per second in some species up to 1700 per second in others. The number of pulses per second may be species specific, in which case the signal can indicate identity. The fish have sensitive electrical receptors which, in addition to their communication function, can also provide navigational information and warning of an approaching predator: they can detect minute distortions of the surrounding electrical field when another animal or object is nearby. In the mormyrid fish species, the receptors are so sensitive that they are temporarily inactivated when the fish produces an electrical pulse. Thus the outgoing pulse does not drown out the receptors and the fish is electrically "deaf" to its own signals.

▽ *The electric fish of Africa and South America produce bursts of electricity to stun their prey, to find their way through the often murky water of their river and lake habitats, and to communicate their location and "ownership" of a hunting territory to other electric fish, whether members of their own species or otherwise.*

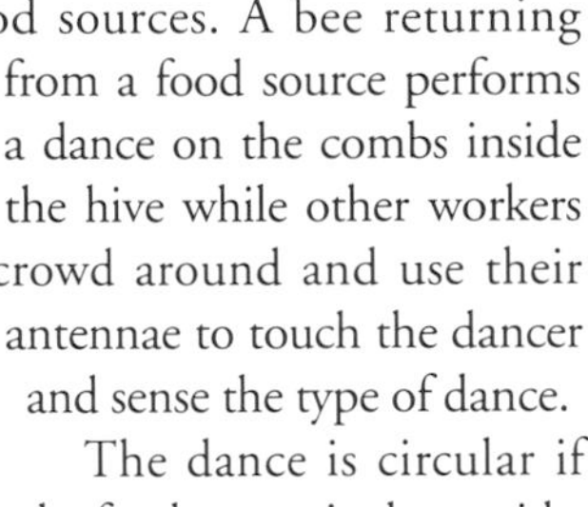

The dance of the honeybee

The honeybee is a highly social animal. Within the darkness of the hive, touch is used to communicate information about food sources. A bee returning from a food source performs a dance on the combs inside the hive while other workers crowd around and use their antennae to touch the dancer and sense the type of dance.

The dance is circular if the food source is close, within about 50 yards (80 m), but more distant sources are indicated by the "waggle" dance, which is in a figure-of-eight. On the straight part of the eight the bee performs a number of waggles. The larger the number of waggles and the faster the dance, the closer the food source is to the hive. The direction of the source from the hive is also indicated, not by a compass, but by the sun. The angle of the straight run on the vertical comb indicates the direction in which the workers have to fly relative to the position of the sun. If the straight part of the dance is aligned vertically and the bee is moving upward as it performs the waggle, the other workers know that they have to fly straight toward the sun. If the straight part of the dance is aligned vertically but the bee is moving downward as it performs the waggle, the workers have to fly away from the sun.

▷ *Tropical tree frogs call to attract a mate, however, they often manage to attract frog-eating bats instead.*

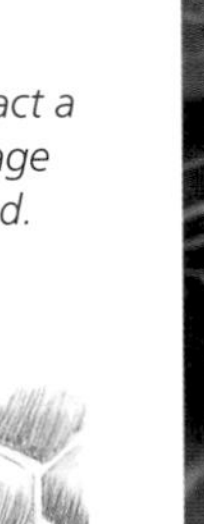

In the darkness of the hive, honeybees rely on touch and patterns of movement to communicate the direction and distance of nectar supplies. A circular dance (top) means food is close, while the speed and number of movements in a figure-of-eight dance (center) indicate the source of food further from the hive. The alignment of both dances shows other workers direction, according to the position of the sun.

Songs and screeches

Animal sounds are very diverse, as are the uses to which sound is put. Frogs, birds, and cicadas can often fill their surroundings with sound, but despite the apparent cacophony there are signals passing between individuals, often between the sexes. The screeches of troops of monkeys are very obvious to us, but there is a wide range of sounds that we are less aware of, such as the sound of marine creatures, or that we simply cannot hear.

The male white-throated sparrow has a characteristic song that is endlessly repeated once spring arrives. This song is part of the territorial display of the male and he will respond to a strange song by flying over to the intruder, singing and displaying. He can distinguish males from other areas who have a different "dialect" and, of course, males of other species, who have a different song pattern. The females do not have territories and do not sing. The structure and size of the brain area where the nerve pathways are associated with the windpipe require the sex hormone signals of a male to develop correctly for singing. A female given appropriate hormone injections may develop singing abilities like the male.

Animal eavesdroppers

One of the assumptions that can be made about communication in general is that the number of participants is frequently three: the sender, the receiver, and the eavesdropper. This is certainly true among animals. Some bats, for instance, are very good at eavesdropping. The frog-eating bat can detect its prey, tropical tree frogs, by their calls. The male Tungara frog calls to attract a mate; unfortunately for the frog, the most effective call for attracting a female is also the most effective at attracting a bat. The call is in two parts, a "whine" and up to three "chucks." The chuck provides very good directional information, so a lone frog often drops this part of the call as a defense against bats, even though without the chuck the call is less attractive to females. A group of frogs calling together reduces the risk of predation for each individual, however, and so in a group the frogs can use the complete song with a reasonable chance of mating and not being eaten. If the night is not too dark the frog can see the bat, stop calling and take evasive action. But on a dark night bats can be very successful at preying on the frogs, plucking them out of the water with their jaws.

For many animals the price of conspicuous signaling seems to be a much greater risk of attracting unwelcome attention. Yet there is obviously no advantage in being superbly camouflaged and invisible to potential mates. There is generally a trade-off between an animal being cryptic and inconspicuous and advertising its presence or attributes to others.

◁ *The frog-eating bat of Central America eavesdrops on male Tungara frogs calling to attract mates, pinpointing the frog's position and gliding in on silent wings to scoop up its prey. Individual frogs must choose between remaining quiet—and missing out on the chance to mate—or taking the risk of being attacked.*

High-Speed Sound

The fastest communication in the insect world is via sound, but it is beyond our range of hearing. The speckled bush cricket is flightless and lives in bushes and trees. The male produces a very short call made up of a few pulses lasting around one thousandth of a second each. If he hears a female reply he continues to call and moves toward her, using her reply as an acoustic beacon. But her reply is very short—usually just one pulse—and the timing of it is crucial: if it does not fall within the time window during which the male expects a reply, he ignores her. This time window is very short: the male expects a reply within about thirty thousandths of a second from his call. This timing is so fast that the female's response has to be a reflex. There simply isn't time for her brain to get involved.

At that sort of speed, the travel time of sound in air becomes important. If the male and female are 3 feet (1 m) apart, the male's sound will take three thousandths of a second to get to the female and her reply will take a similar time to get back to him.

The signal itself is so short that it cannot carry much information. The female just listens for a short sound on the right frequency and replies to that. If her reply stimulates further short sounds, she assumes that it is a male, and of course it usually is. However, if you click two of your fingernails together rapidly you will generate enough ultrasound to fool a female speckled bush cricket and she will reply to you.

It is interesting to speculate on why these calls are so short, as you would expect a beacon signal to be a long one. One possible explanation is that predators able to hear ultrasound, such as bats, might be able to home in on a longer sound and eat the singer.

◁ *The male speckled bush cricket uses ultrasound to find a mate, emitting calls that last no longer than a thousandth of a second—and providing the female with a similarly short "window" in which she can reply. This high-speed communication may have evolved as a defense against predators such as bats.*

ATTACK AND DEFENSE

Dr. Felicity A. Huntingford

Why do animals fight, given that combat is costly in terms of time, energy, and the risk of injury? There are essentially two main reasons: in self-defense, to protect an animal or its young against a direct threat; or to gain exclusive or preferential access to some valued resource.

The former is most clearly seen when the animal concerned is attacked by a predator (the "cornered rat" syndrome) or an attacking conspecific or when its young are threatened, either by a predator or a member of its own species. In such cases, the animals often attack extremely fiercely, using all available weapons as vigorously as possible.

The resources that animals fight over include mates, food, and territory. What happens during fights depends on the value of the disputed resource and on the risk each participant runs of getting injured. Many fights involve threat displays that emphasize or advertise an animal's size or weaponry and therefore intimidate other animals into giving up before the fight escalates. But often a full-scale fight does develop, particularly if the rivals are well matched in size and fighting ability or if they are contesting a very valuable resource. Such fights can end in injury, and even death.

Displays, threats, and escalation

Mountain or bighorn sheep, like many other species, have a repertoire of behavior patterns that they deploy during fights. In general, fights between mountain sheep start with an exchange of low-key actions performed at a distance—threat displays. Many threat displays have the effect of emphasizing or advertising an animal's size, such as when the animal stands side on, or even of making the performer seem larger than it actually is, such as when some species raise their hair. Threat displays also commonly expose the performer's weapons—in this case horns—to a rival.

Above: For a male red fox, control over territory ensures an adequate food supply for himself, his mate, and their several cubs. Again, fights between rivals for the same territory consist mainly of displays of strength and endurance.
Left: Male elephant seals defend a group of females by engaging in fights with their challenger which rapidly escalate to become vicious and bloody battles.

▷ *The skulls of male mountain sheep are reinforced to provide strength for territorial fights with other rams, and the neck muscles are very large, allowing rams literally to lock horns without the risk of dislocating their necks.*

Submissive displays often have the opposite properties, and reduce the chances that the animal concerned will be attacked; they therefore serve as an important behavioral defense.

Initially, direct physical contact is relatively harmless and involves such actions as kicking, but as the fight progresses intense and potentially dangerous actions such as clashing come into play. This progressive increase in the intensity of a fight is described as escalation. Conflicts can be resolved at any point in the escalation sequence if one participant retreats or fails to retaliate.

CLASH OF THE TITANS

Adult male mountain sheep are very large animals, weighing up to 300 pounds (135 kg)—more than 40 percent larger than the maximum size for adult females. When they fight, the conflicts can be long and fierce. The fiercest fights occur between rams aged 6–8 years, especially when the opponents are of equal horn and body size. The biologist who has studied this species most intensively, Valerius Geist, has described the fights as "slugging and wrestling matches" in which "rams whirl around each other, try to keep their horns pointed at the opponent (as a defense measure), and attempt to crash into the opponent's side wherever possible. They hit out sideways with their heads, push each other around with chest and shoulders, [and] butt each other wherever possible while trying to avoid the blows of the other."

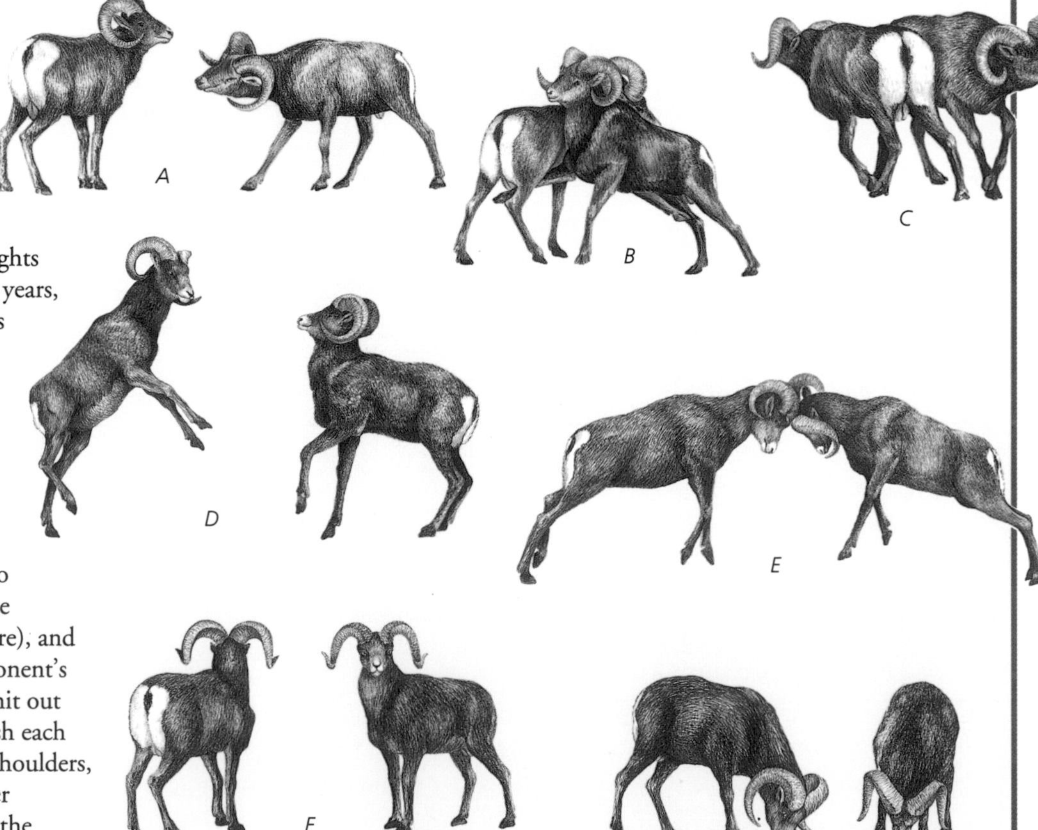

A fight between rams typically begins when one ram approaches another with his head pulled back and lowered, his ears folded back and his eyes narrowed, and his horns directed toward the opponent in a low stretch (A). The rams then exchange a series of kicks aimed at the chest and belly, accompanied by growls (B). Abruptly, both males pull away and take up a low stretch (C) before rearing onto their hind legs (D) then dropping with great force into a head-on clash (E). One ram often takes advantage of higher ground to gain greater impact with this drop. A clash is often followed by mutual presenting (F), in which the rams stand side by side and display their horns to each other, or a short bout of feeding (G), after which the rams return to kicking. This cycle may be repeated many times, until one ram fails to retaliate and either submits or flees.

△ A male European stag beetle uses his greatly enlarged chelicerae, or nippers, seeking to lift his opponent off the ground.

Weapons and shields

The dictionary definition of a weapon is "an instrument of any kind used in warfare or combat to attack and overcome an enemy" (Oxford English Dictionary). Many animals have strong hard structures used to manipulate the environment in a variety of ways, such as for digging into the ground, or for acquiring food, or for running. In many cases these structures are deployed as weapons during fights, although animals such as rattlesnakes, which have lethal fangs for dispatching prey, do not use these weapons against another animal of the same species. In other species, weapons are specialized structures used only during fights, where they serve both to maintain contact with an opponent and to push, batter, gore, or otherwise injure it.

◁ Sea cucumbers have evolved a unique way of deterring predators. When attacked they forcibly expel sticky, toxic outgrowths of the hindgut from the anus—an arresting and very discouraging demonstration of their unpalatability.

Given this awesome array of weaponry, it is not surprising that animals possess a variety of adaptations, both physical and behavioral, that reduce their chances of serious injury during fights or when attacked by a predator. When sea cucumbers are disturbed, special tubular outgrowths of the wall of the hindgut are expelled rapidly through the anus; these are both sticky and toxic and, understandably, discourage potential predators from attacking. When captured by a predator such as a toad, bombardier beetles release a chemical that is so evil-tasting that the beetle is immediately spat out. Wading birds such as the black-capped stilt lead potential predators away from their brood by feigning an injury such as a broken wing. A wolf defeated in a fight can avoid being attacked by its victorious companion by taking up a posture similar to that used by pups when begging for food from their parents.

The male mountain sheep is a dramatic manifestation of the simultaneous demands of attack and defense. The horns themselves are formidable weapons, but are structured in such a way that they can be used defensively, to parry an opponent's blows. Rams may reduce the impact of a blow by turning to receive it on the head (which is protected by thick bone) rather than on the more vulnerable flanks.

The costs of fighting

The adverse consequences of animal fights, besides the obvious risk of injury or death, include a considerable waste of precious energy and time. Many animal conflicts are resolved without full escalation, even though the animals concerned possess potentially lethal weapons; for this reason, animal fights used to be viewed as harmless trials of strength. But it is now clear that, in certain circumstances, and notwithstanding defensive behavior, weapons are used to injure and kill during animal fights.

One study of mountain sheep during two rutting seasons found that small rams were telescoped by the force of direct charges by larger opponents, horn tips were often broken, and a variety of cuts, tears, and bruises were commonly incurred during fights. In addition to these relatively minor complaints, almost 50 percent of males sustained serious injury during the study period. Figures for a range of other species tell the same story.

One particular fight between rutting male mountain sheep lasted more than 25 hours —time that the participants could potentially have spent doing something else, such as eating or mating—and left both participants exhausted. More precise studies estimate that fighting can raise the metabolic rate considerably above that of resting animals. In velvet swimming crabs, respiration rates show a tenfold increase during fights. Immediately after an intense fight, a crab's capacity for vigorous activity may be compromised; in addition, the energy put into fighting is not available for other purposes, such as growth and reproductive investment. Using an analogy from economics, these adverse consequences are referred to as "costs of fighting."

▽ Often involved in vigorous fights with other females over males, the female jacana or lotus bird is up to 75 percent larger than the male. She must also bear the energy costs of nesting, laying, and incubating eggs and provides her young with at least half their food and the bulk of their care.

The benefits of fighting

Given such high costs, fighting must confer some compensatory benefits. There are essentially just two general reasons why animals fight: in some cases, fighting serves to protect an animal or its young against a direct threat; in other cases, animals fight in order to gain exclusive or preferential access to some valued resource. The more valuable the resource, the fiercer the fight—and the higher the benefit to the winner.

Many male animals compete for access to fertile females, and the winners are more likely to gain matings. In general, because a single male (of whatever species) can potentially produce sufficient sperm to fertilize many females, the latter tend to be in short supply. Consequently, fights between males over females are common; this is what stag beetles

▷ Some species of highly social blackbirds have little incentive to fight over territory or mates. Food, however, is a different matter, and blackbirds of either sex will battle fiercely over scarce food supplies in winter, with the loser possibly starving to death.

Animal Arsenals

The essential feature of an animal's weapon is that when deployed forcibly it is capable of damaging the tissue of another animal, causing pain and injury. The aim is to incapacitate the rival, or at least force it to retreat. Many "weapons" used in fighting are in fact hard and/or sharp organs which are primarily used for another purpose. These include the proboscis of the ragworm and the horn of the stag beetle, both used mainly for burrowing into the earth; the sting of the honeybee, originally used during egg laying; the club-like tentacles of the anemone and the beak of the young eagle, both used during feeding, and the hooves of the zebra, used for locomotion.

Some animals, however, develop completely new structures which are used only during fighting. These include the hooked upper jaw (or kype) of the male Coho salmon and the antlers of red deer stags. Termite soldiers use chemical weapons, squirting glue from the elongated proboscis at high pressure and with great precision. This glue poisons enemies as well as entangling them, and is effective even against relatively large attackers such as birds. In a few cases, particularly among primates, inanimate objects are used as defensive weapons; chimpanzees, for example, are known to attack leopards with sticks.

▽ *The only animals that use inanimate objects (such as sticks or rocks) to defend themselves or to attack predators are primates. Most animals rely on "weapons" from their own anatomy: zebras use their hard hooves to defend themselves against rivals as well as for locomotion.*

◁ *Adult birds of prey rely on their powerful talons to capture prey, but use their sharp beaks to dismember food or to defend themselves in territorial conflicts. Nestlings threaten potential predators with a gaping beak, though their undeveloped musculature makes it unlikely that they would be able to inflict any damage.*

△ *When rivals for territory or mates are evenly matched, actual combat is required before a fight can be resolved. Nevertheless, bull elephants rarely use their formidable tusks to injure each other, relying instead on strength, tenacity, and endurance.*

▽ *The fiercest fights take place over resources that can make the difference between life and death. Polar bears often have to battle for scarce and uncertain food supplies on the barren Arctic ice: the winner will still have enough energy left to search for food, while the loser faces a much less certain future.*

use their horns for, and gladiator frogs their sharp thumbs. And it is one reason why males are often larger and better armored than females. But there are exceptions to this rule. Females as well as males may fight over other valuable but limited resources. When anemones club each other, they are fighting over feeding space; when young raptors attack and kill their small siblings they are fighting over the food that their parents bring; and when funnel web spiders attack intruders into their territory they are, in effect, defending a supply of insect prey.

The complexity of so many animal fights is the result of the simultaneous needs of attack (to increase the chances of gaining the disputed resource) and defense (to reduce the risk of being injured). In response to these conflicting requirements, animals adjust their behavior during fights according to the value of the disputed resource, their chances of winning, and their risk of getting injured. The fiercest fights take place over resources that confer large fitness benefits on the winner. In arid regions of the United States, good feeding sites for funnel web spiders are few and far between. Spiders captured at such sites are very much more aggressive than those of the same species captured in wetter areas where food is more abundant.

Well-matched rivals

The probability of winning a fight as opposed to getting injured depends mainly on how well an animal is able to fight compared to its rival, and this in turn is determined mainly, but not exclusively, by their relative size. In mountain sheep, fights are commonest, longest, and most intense between rams that are more or less equally matched in body size and horn development, suggesting that smaller, poorly armed individuals avoid fights or give up on them at an early stage. This would be in the interest of the loser as well as the winner, since the inevitable result—victory to the better fighter—can be achieved at minimum cost to both.

Current theory sees animal fights as a process of gradual acquisition of information about the rival's fighting ability, with less effective individuals giving up once they have discovered their relative status. This explains why threat displays tend to emphasize the size of the performer's body and weapons. Even so, displays performed at a distance provide less direct and less accurate information about fighting ability than direct contact between opponents. So when there is little to choose between the rivals, escalated combat is required before a fight can be resolved.

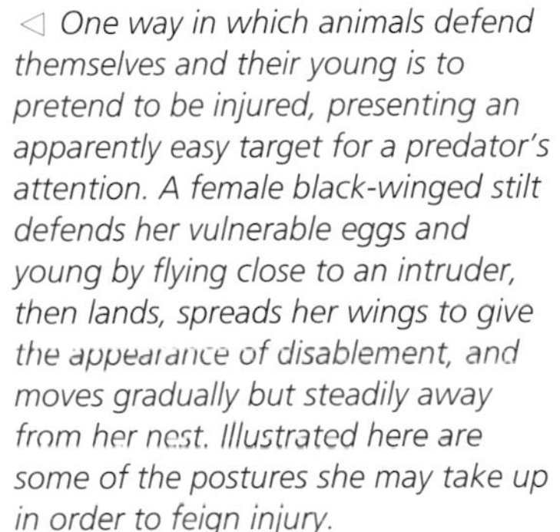

◁ *One way in which animals defend themselves and their young is to pretend to be injured, presenting an apparently easy target for a predator's attention. A female black-winged stilt defends her vulnerable eggs and young by flying close to an intruder, then lands, spreads her wings to give the appearance of disablement, and moves gradually but steadily away from her nest. Illustrated here are some of the postures she may take up in order to feign injury.*

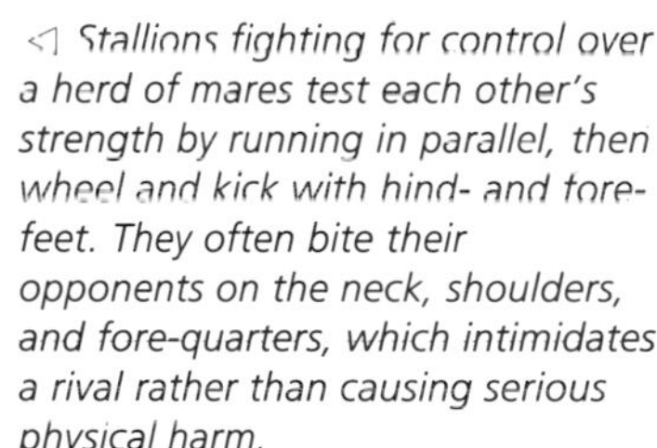

◁ *Stallions fighting for control over a herd of mares test each other's strength by running in parallel, then wheel and kick with hind- and fore-feet. They often bite their opponents on the neck, shoulders, and fore-quarters, which intimidates a rival rather than causing serious physical harm.*

▽ *Where there is little to be gained from actual combat, display is the most common form of both attack and defense. The frill-necked lizard attempts to bluff predators and rivals alike by spreading its neck frill, hoping to intimidate by a sudden increase in apparent size.*

HIERARCHY

Dr. Marion J. Hall

Wherever animals live in groups, there is inevitably conflict over who gets any resources—such as food or mates—that are in short supply. Fighting involves risking injury or death, so it is not worth going into battle unless there is some certainty of winning or the resource being fought for is very valuable. Once two individuals in the same social group have fought each other, therefore, and a winner and a loser have emerged, there is generally no point in fighting again because the outcome is probably going to be the same. The loser might as well defer to the winner. The winner has become dominant to the loser and the loser in turn has become subordinate to the winner.

The dominance hierarchy

In a social group with a stable composition, all the members of the group are likely to know each other, and dominance relationships can be established between every possible pair of animals. As a result, a clear dominance hierarchy emerges and individuals can be ranked in order of the number of other animals they are dominant to. One individual—often called the "alpha" animal—dominates all the others, another dominates all the others except the alpha, and so on, down to the "omega" animal, which is subordinate to all the others and dominant to none. Individuals toward the top of the hierarchy are often described as "high ranking," "high status," or simply "dominant," though the last term—while a convenient shorthand—is not strictly correct because dominance is not a property of a single individual but only of the *relationship* between a particular pair of individuals. Similarly, the individuals toward the bottom of the hierarchy of any group are said to be "low ranking," "low status," or simply "subordinate."

Above: Older animals in any group tend to dominate juveniles because the young animals are smaller and less well developed. Juveniles adopt "submissive" behavior, like this young dingo with the group's dominant adult male.
Left: Once a hierarchy has been established in a group of animals, such as these hippos, threat displays are generally sufficient to maintain the status quo.

▽ *When a receptive female baboon "presents" herself to a male to solicit mating, she looks back over her shoulder at him (left). When a subordinate baboon, male or female, encounters a threatening dominant baboon, it adopts the same general behavior of presenting its rump to the higher-ranking animal, but the expression on its face is one of fear (center). This "fear grin" (right) is used to appease a more dominant animal. Monkeys and apes, particularly chimpanzees, use many facial expressions to communicate.*

The concept of a dominance hierarchy was developed in the 1920s from observations on domestic hens, which can usually be ordered into a highly linear hierarchy based on who pecks whom. For this reason, the dominance hierarchy was originally called a "pecking order," a term which has become absorbed into everyday English. Since then, dominance hierarchies have been observed in many different species. They seem to be present in most social vertebrates, though the degree of linearity varies enormously. They have also been found in certain invertebrate species, including some crickets, ants, wasps, and shrimp.

Establishing the hierarchy

A dominance relationship can be established simply by individuals assessing each other's fighting ability every time they meet and then behaving accordingly; attack if your opponent is weaker, submit if you are. This system does not require the animals to have any ability to recognize each other as individuals, but it is unstable because closely matched individuals will usually end up fighting, and the outcome between a particular pair may vary. But where individuals are able to recognize other members of their group and then to learn from their previous encounters with those individuals, a very stable dominance hierarchy can be established. Consequently, dominance hierarchies are most clearly seen in social groups with a composition that changes little over time.

Learning may play another role in the establishment of dominance status. It has been suggested that animals may "learn" to be dominant or subordinate. Thus an individual that has just won a fight may go in to a fight with another individual expecting to win, and may end up winning simply because of the extra confidence this gives it. Conversely, a loser may continue to lose because it has lost confidence and expects to lose. So, whether an individual ends up with high or low status could depend, to some extent, on its very first encounter.

Keeping The Ranks In Order

Dominance relationships are usually maintained by occasional threats directed by the dominant toward the subordinate—a sort of "reminder" of their relationship—but actual fights are very rare. Subordinates often avoid individuals dominant to them; if an encounter does take place, they may show appeasement or submissive displays, which demonstrate their acceptance of the other individual's dominance over them. In many species of monkey, for example, subordinates, whether male or female, show submission by turning their back on a dominant individual and presenting their rump, in the same way that a receptive female does when soliciting mating from a male. Monkeys and apes also make a facial gesture rather like a grin, which acts to appease a dominant. In many animals, dominants and subordinates can be distinguished not only by their behavior but by differences in their general posture and even, in some cases, their plumage or color. The skin of the green anole lizard, for example, becomes darker after losing a fight, and the darkness of the skin is correlated with the lizard's dominance rank.

"Fear grin" of chimpanzee

Sexual (far left) and submissive (left) presentation.

△ *In many social animal species, such as wolves, the dominance hierarchy is a strong determinant of behavior within the group. Dominant animals behave very differently from their subordinates; here, the low-ranking wolf on the right shows submissive behavior—in its facial expression and posture—to the dominant wolf on the left.*

In many species, however, dominance status does seem to be related to physical characteristics that are likely to influence fighting ability, such as body size or the development of "weapons." As a result, the larger sex—often, but not always, the male—tends to dominate the smaller.

Similarly, older individuals tend to dominate younger individuals because dominance relationships tend to be established early in life, when the juvenile is smaller and less well developed than older members of the group.

But status can also be "inherited" in some species. In baboons and macaque monkeys, for example, a female's rank is determined by that of her mother. Her daughters slot in just below her in the hierarchy, but in reverse order of age—in other words her youngest daughter is next to her in rank, followed by her second-youngest daughter, and so on. This is because the mother will tend to intervene to help her daughters in any aggressive interactions they become involved in, but she is most likely to help her youngest daughter and least likely to help the eldest.

Moving up and down the ranks

Status is not static. In baboons and macaques, a young female will move down the hierarchy every time a younger sister is born. Individuals also move up the hierarchy as they get older, as those at the top die, and as new youngsters come in at the bottom. Sometimes, a role reversal occurs —one individual "challenges" another to which it is normally subordinate and, after a period of fighting, becomes dominant if it wins, or remains subordinate if it loses.

"Coalitions" can be formed in which two or more subordinate animals gang up to beat one individual that would normally dominate them when separate. This kind of co-operative behavior is particularly common among primates.

There can be seasonal variations in status, too. For example, throughout much of the year, red deer live in groups, either bachelor groups consisting of all males, or matriarchal groups consisting of females and their younger offspring. Both male and female groups have a fairly linear dominance hierarchy, related to age and body size. Males lock antlers and push against each other

The Element of Chance

A strictly linear dominance hierarchy, in which animals can be ordered from alpha individual to omega individual, is relatively rare. It can happen, particularly where one animal becomes dominant over another because it is bigger or stronger, and this pattern is repeated for all the other pairs of individuals in the group. The order of dominance will then reflect the order of size or strength of the members of the group.

But often an element of chance creeps in. Imagine three male baboons A, B and C. C might by chance beat A in a fight even though A is bigger than him. B, on the other hand, being between A and C in size, is beaten by A and himself beats C, as might be expected. This gives rise to what amounts to a "triangular relationship" between the three males rather than a straightforward linear hierarchy.

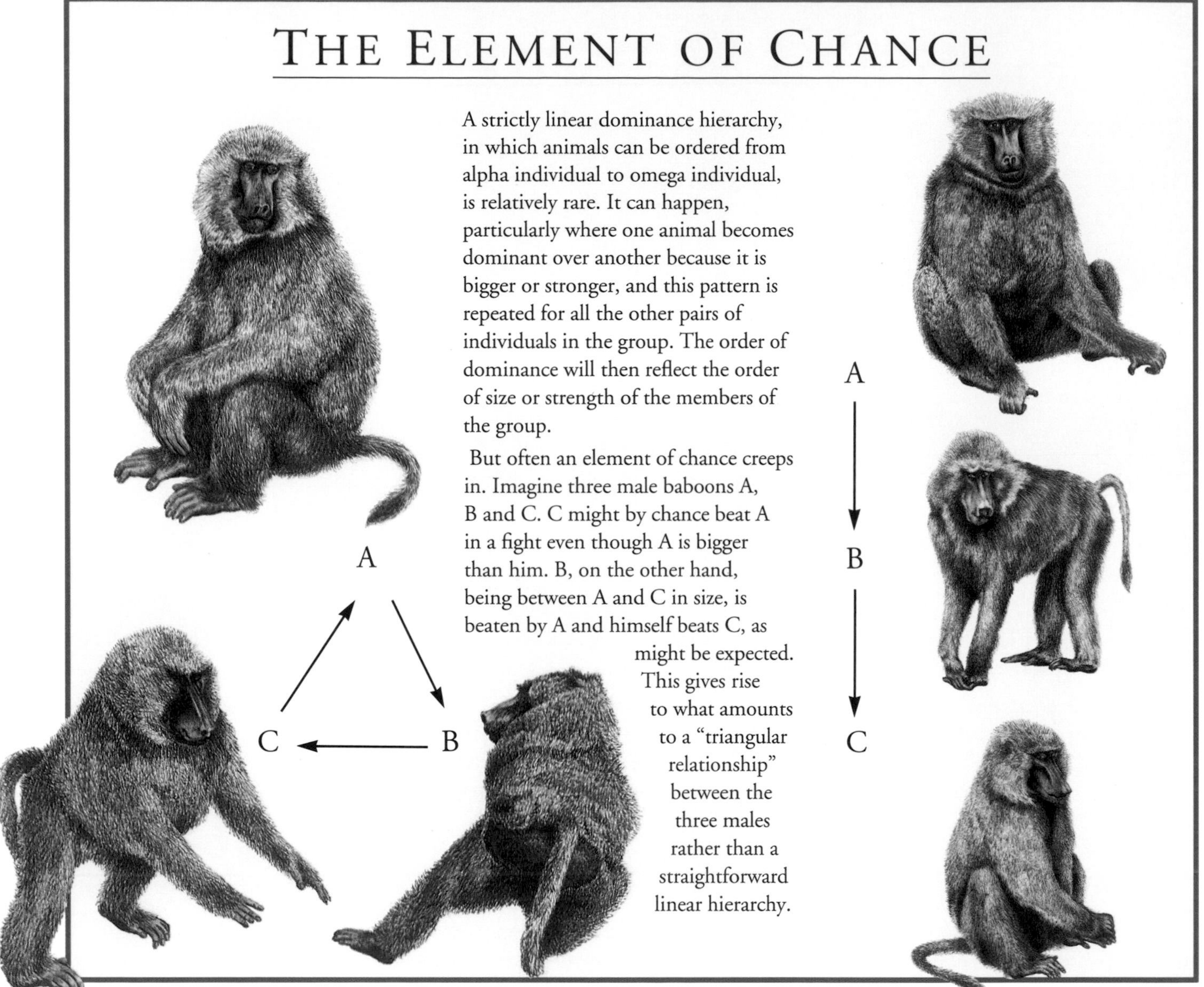

△ *If the outcome of the initial encounter between two animals depends to some extent on chance, then triangular relationships such as that shown on the left can develop, instead of the linear order of dominance (right) expected on the basis of size or some other feature that contributes to fighting prowess.*

when they fight, and one male will often threaten another by lowering his antlers at him. But deer lose their antlers—their main fighting weapon—every year and grow a new set to replace them. When a red deer male loses his antlers he tends to drop down the hierarchy. As other males lose theirs, they also drop down, slotting in so that, by the time all the males have lost their antlers, the same hierarchy is seen as when they all had them.

The importance of time and place

Many species live in hierarchical groups for only part of the year. Red deer males, for example, leave their bachelor groups during the fall breeding season—the rut. Each individual male tries to defend a group of females he can mate with, by fighting any other male who challenges him for possession. Similarly, many birds flock during winter but will defend separate breeding territories in spring and summer.

Dominance among territory owners is usually an all-or-nothing thing—a territorial animal is dominant over all others on its own territory, but as soon as it crosses its boundary, it becomes subordinate to its neighbor. For this reason, strict territoriality and hierarchical groups are sometimes regarded as distinct types of social organization. But, in fact, they are probably

◁ *The fabled vanity of the peacock is most obvious in the least dominant cock in a flock—it is necessary for them to "work" harder to attract a mate.*

▽ *A map of a peafowl lek, showing the main display site of each male in the group (represented by the letters A to L), which is situated roughly in the center of his breeding territory. The rank order of the top five males at four different feeding sites in the lek, shown by arrows, demonstrates that each male's status varies according to where in the lek he is. The further away he is from his own display site and breeding territory, the lower his status. Thus, at feeding site 2, peacock K is the top-ranker; at feeding sites 1 and 4, he does not even rank in the top five.*

more properly regarded as the two extremes of a continuum. Sometimes, a territory is held by a group within which there is a dominance hierarchy, or at least one dominant individual who dominates several subordinates.

Whether a species is territorial or group-living can also depend on population density. At low density, house mice and cockroaches are territorial but, as density increases, the territorial system breaks down; the amount of fighting necessary to defend a territory increases until the risks involved become too great. Instead, a dominance hierarchy is established in which the good fighters who were able to defend territories at low density become the dominants.

Winter flocks of several bird species show a linear dominance hierarchy, but the order of individuals within that hierarchy changes with the whereabouts of the flock, often in relation to the position of breeding territories. Peafowl, for example, have a breeding system in which males defend small display territories within a traditional breeding area—the lek—to which females are attracted to mate. Outside the breeding season, peacocks tend to move around together in small unstable flocks. The territorial males from a particular lek always show a linear dominance hierarchy, but the order of males within that hierarchy depends on whereabouts on the lek the hierarchy is observed. Basically, each male's rank depends on how far he is from the display territory he holds in the spring—in an aggressive interaction between two males, the one nearer to his own territory will usually be the winner.

The fruits of success

Depending on the species, high-ranking animals gain a variety of benefits. Priority of access to food is common—for example, high-status woodpigeons have higher feeding rates than low-status birds, and dominant red deer can displace subordinates from preferred feeding sites. There can be other benefits, too. Dominant willow tits feed in the safest parts of pine trees, high up and where the leaves are thick enough to hide them, forcing subordinates to go lower down or where the leaves are sparse, where they are more vulnerable to predators, such as hawks and owls.

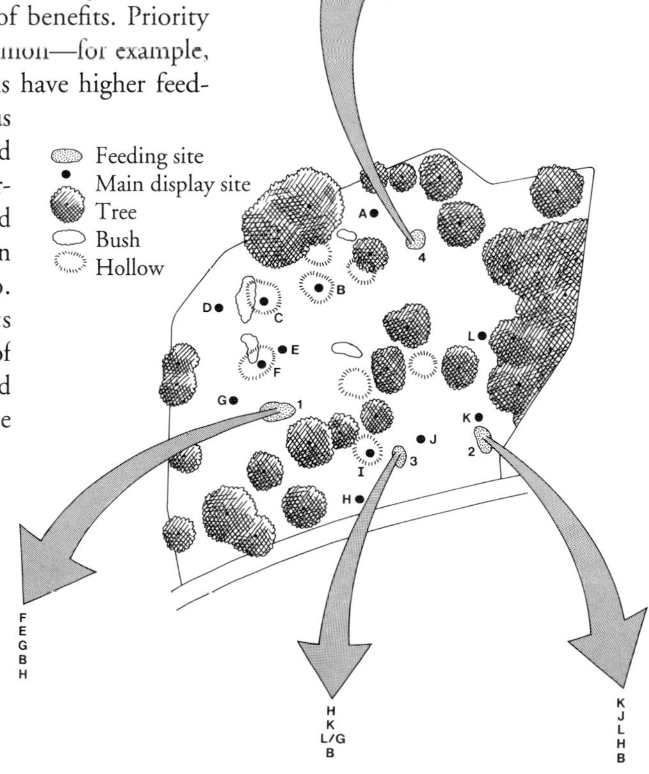

High-ranking animals can also be more successful when the time comes to reproduce. In red deer, buffalo and elephant seals, among many other species, how many mates a male can get is closely related to his status. Even if subordinates copulate as often as dominants, they may get less access to the female during her most fertile period.

In some animals, only the alpha individual in a group breeds at all. A pack of wolves or African wild dogs usually contains just one breeding pair—the top-ranking female and the top-ranking male. Subordinate female wolves may ovulate and court males, but will only produce a litter if the alpha female is removed. Should a subordinate wild dog produce a litter, few if any of the pups will survive because of harassment by the dominant female.

▽ *Hierarchical ranking is usually, but not always, related to size. In this photograph, the smaller macaque appears to be dominant to the larger.*

Compensating for low status

It is easy to see how a dominant individual can benefit from the hierarchy system—it will often have priority of access to food, mates, resting places, and other resources. But what does a subordinate get out of the system? It may, of course, just be making the best of a bad job. It cannot beat the dominant in a fight, so it may as well give in straight away. And, with time, it will move up the hierarchy, so it may eventually enjoy the benefits of being dominant.

It has been suggested, however, that subordinates may not do so badly out of the relationship. The dominant animal may get better access to resources, but it has to "live up to its reputation" by being willing to fight if challenged. It may, as a result, run a greater risk of being killed or injured. In some species, high-ranking males play a greater role in defending the group against predators or rival groups. The subordinate, on the other hand, while it may have less access to resources, does not get involved in fights or other dangerous activities. The costs to each balance out to some extent.

Subordinate animals can sometimes compensate for their lower status—by cooperating with each other to defeat a dominant animal, for example. They can also adopt "alternative strategies" to help increase their opportunities to mate. Subordinate males in some species, for instance, mimic females, behaviorally and sometimes physically, so that they can get close enough to females to mate with them without attracting aggressive behavior from the other, more dominant males. In other species they practice "satellite" behavior. For example, some subordinate male frogs, toads, and crickets wait silently near a dominant male that is calling to attract females. The satellite male is sometimes able to intercept and mate with females that were heading for the caller. In bighorn sheep, dominant males wait in areas where herds of ewes congregate and then court and defend receptive females. Occasionally, dominant males will battle each other for access to a female; when this happens, subordinate satellite males try to rush past them and copulate quickly with the female —not too impossible, as copulation only lasts a few seconds in bighorn sheep!

Badges of Status

In many species of birds, individuals vary greatly in the pattern or color of their plumage. In several cases, these variations seem to act as signals of dominance status. The wider the black stripe down the front of the breast of a great tit, the larger the black throat patch (bib) in a male house sparrow, or the brighter the plumage of a greenfinch, the higher the status of the bird concerned when the species flock together during winter. In contests over food, for example, a great tit with a narrow breast stripe will give way to one with a broad breast stripe. Plumage variations that signal dominance in this way have been called badges of status. The term has also been applied to some lizard species that use body markings to signal dominance.

The unusual feature of this system is that the width of the breast stripe, the size of the bib, the brightness of the plumage, or whatever aspect acts as the badge, tends to bear no relation to the fighting ability of the bird. If two birds do end up fighting, it is not possible to predict which one will win on the basis of their plumage. The badge seems to be used by the birds as a conventional way of settling a dispute—much as two people might toss a coin to decide who gets the last cookie on a plate.

It would seem easy to cheat the system—why don't great tits with narrow breast stripes simply produce more black pigment and increase the size of their badge? Surely, the costs of making more pigment would be small and the benefits to be gained in terms of access to food would be large? There are two possible reasons why birds do not cheat. It could be that the costs of producing the badge are much greater than they appear, and/or that the benefits to be gained are not as great as might be supposed, so that costs and benefits balance out and individuals with small badges in fact do just as well as those with large ones. There is some evidence that in great tits, large badges are associated with a higher metabolic rate and increased heart size; if this is the case, large badges will be costly because more food will be needed to maintain the high metabolic rate. The badges of several species also involve carotenoid pigments, which can only be obtained from the small quantities present in certain foods—the brightness of a greenfinch, for example, depends on how much yellow carotenoid it can accumulate. This may involve time spent searching for particular types of food. It may also be the case that birds with large badges have to be prepared to back up their signal by fighting if necessary; they therefore run a greater risk of injury.

There is also evidence that the benefits the badge confers may not be so great. Badges seem to be used when the value of the resource being disputed is not very high—when there is plenty of food around, for example, and it is easy to go and feed somewhere else if seen off by someone with a bigger badge. When food becomes scarce, the badge system breaks down.

Badges are also more often used in large, unstable flocks, where the birds are unlikely to get to know each other. There is no opportunity to establish a dominance hierarchy in the usual way, so birds "toss a coin" to settle disputes that are not worth fighting over. In small, stable flocks of birds, dominance relationships are set up on the basis of fighting ability, and badges are much less important.

△ *House sparrows*
◁ *Great tit*

LIVING WITH OTHER ANIMALS

Dr. Angela K. Turner

When animals live in groups they usually do so with members of their own species, and are then variously referred to as herds, flocks, and so on. Some relationships, however, are struck between quite different animals. There are three categories of such associations: parasitism, commensal relationships, and symbiosis. In parasitism, only one partner in the relationship benefits by it, while the other is harmed in some way. Often, severe infestations of parasites can cause the death of the unwilling host. Only one partner benefits in commensal relationships, too, but here the other animal is unharmed; in fact, it is unaffected.

Cattle egrets feed on insects disturbed from the vegetation by grazing cattle, which don't gain—or lose—anything themselves.

Commensal relationships are rare, however; much more common are mutually beneficial relationships such as those between fish and cleaner fish. These associations are known as symbiosis or mutualism.

Just good friends

Some species live together in very close relationships. Anemone fish, for instance, dwell safe among the tentacles of sea anemones that would sting any predators trying to attack the fish. The anemone fish is not stung itself because it is covered in a slime from the anemone which inhibits it from stinging. The anemone is protected by its partner from foraging fish such as the butterfly fish, which would nibble the anemone's tentacles. The anemone also eats some of its partner's food.

Some anemones have a special relationship with hermit crabs. The crabs seek out anemones and place them on their shell. The anemone feeds on leftovers from the crab's meals, and the crab in turn is defended by the stinging tentacles of the anemone.

Above: Hermit crabs living on coral reefs "plant" stinging anemones on their shells for protection, while the anemone feeds on leftovers from the crab's meals.
Left: Anemone fish coat themselves with slime from their hosts, dwelling safe among stinging tentacles that would kill an intruder; the fish chases away predators, such as butterfly fish, that browse on the anemone's tentacles.

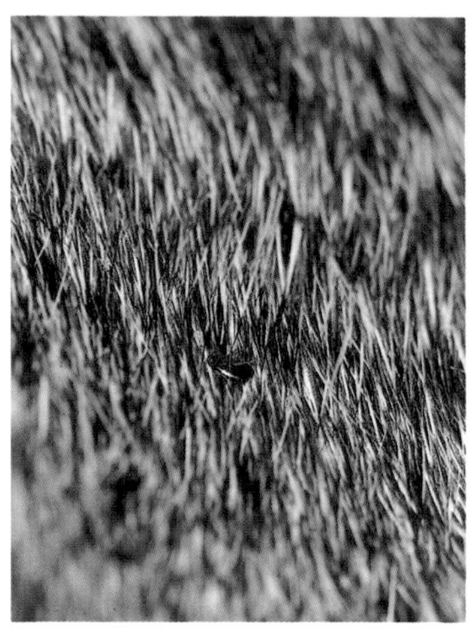

△ In a few cases, humans have used animal parasites to control pests. Rabbit fleas time their own reproduction to coincide with their hosts' breeding cycles; a fact exploited to help spread the viral disease myxomatosis, which has helped reduce the numbers of wild rabbits in, for example, Australia.

Parasites and their hosts

Parasites, in contrast, exploit their hosts. They live on the surface of or inside another animal. Because they are dependent on their hosts for food and shelter, parasites do not usually kill them, as a predator would —at least, not until the parasite has no further need of them. The lives of parasite and host are often closely matched. Rabbit fleas time their breeding to coincide with that of their hosts, so that their offspring will have plenty of new hosts of their own.

A parasite may specialize in one type of host or use two or more different species. The herring gull fluke, for example, lives part of its life cycle in a periwinkle and part in a fish. The adult fluke breeds in the gull's intestines, so its eggs pass out with the bird's droppings into the water. The eggs hatch into a stage called a miracidium—a free-swimming form—which has to find a mollusc host. Once there, it develops into another stage, the cercaria. This stage seeks out a fish in which it encysts and waits for the fish to be eaten by another bird.

Some parasites change their hosts' behavior to their own advantage, making it easier for the parasite to move to the next host. The immature parasite may need its present host to be eaten by another host species in order to mature and complete its life cycle. One flatworm species infects the eyes of dace, impairing their vision. The fish feed less efficiently and spend more time near the surface of the water, where they are more susceptible to being eaten by a bird, which is the parasite's next host. And mice infected with nematodes, which damage their muscles, become sluggish and vulnerable to being caught by a predator, increasing the chances of the nematode being transmitted. Female mice stay in their nest much of the time when they have pups but when infected with nematodes they are less inclined to breed and so continue to be at risk from carnivores, the next host.

As well as changing its behavior, a parasite may change the host's appearance and make it more conspicuous. The flatworms that infect dace make the fish look darker. Another flatworm species infects the tentacles of a snail, making them appear brightly striped, perhaps to attract a predator and so pass on the parasite.

Brood parasites and kleptoparasites

A brood parasite usurps the parental efforts of its host rather than its body—it lays its eggs in its host's nest and leaves the host to rear its offspring. Sometimes, as in the European cuckoo, the host's offspring are killed; in other cases, as in the cowbirds, the parasite and the host offspring grow up together. But the parasite and host chicks compete for food, so fewer hosts survive than in nests without parasites.

Some animals are kleptoparasites, stealing food from another species. Skuas are aerial pirates, attacking smaller seabirds and forcing them to give up their beakload of fish, and blackheaded gulls rob lapwings of hard-won earthworms. Spiders' webs

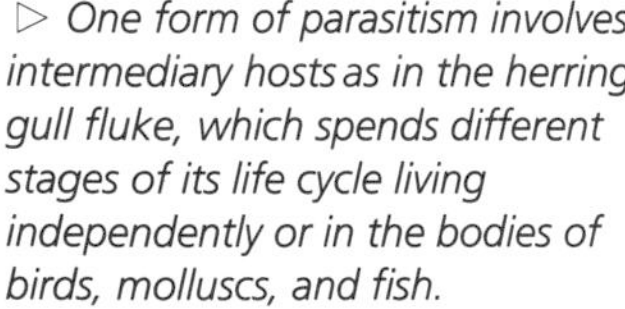

▷ One form of parasitism involves intermediary hosts as in the herring gull fluke, which spends different stages of its life cycle living independently or in the bodies of birds, molluscs, and fish.

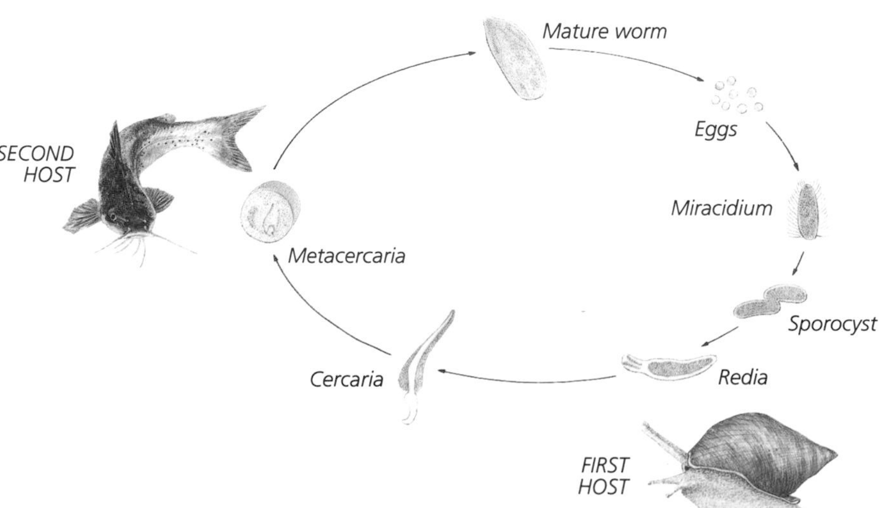

THE HORNBILLS AND THE MONGOOSE

Hornbills in Africa have a very close and mutually beneficial feeding relationship with dwarf mongooses. These birds are very vigilant and warn the mongooses of danger, leaving them more time to hunt. The mongooses lead the way on hunting trips, flushing insects and small reptiles which the hornbills behind them then catch.

The relationship is so close that each morning the hornbills will perch near the mongooses' sleeping site, usually a termite mound, and wait for them to emerge. If the mongooses are late, the birds land on the mound and give a loud call down one of the shafts to wake them up. And if the hornbills are late coming, the mongooses are wary of venturing out to forage until they arrive.

△ *One of the most impressive examples of mutualism—where two species both benefit from living or working together—is between African hornbills (above) and mongooses (left). The hornbills rely on the mongooses to find food, while the mongooses rely on the hornbills to warn them of danger.*

are a particularly easy source of prey, already trapped and trussed in silk, and often predigested by the spider. Scorpion flies and polistine wasps often venture onto webs to steal entangled prey. And one species of bug lives permanently on webs, feeding on insects already overpowered by the spider. Some spiders will even steal entangled or predigested insects they find in the webs of other species.

Mutually beneficial relationships

Many feeding and nesting associations are to the mutual benefit of the different species involved. Some birds, such as titmice or, in the Neotropics, antbirds, form mixed-species flocks—together they can find and harvest food and watch for predators more efficiently than they could if each species formed its own flock. Some species locate and flush food for others, while the more noisy and alert species, such as Carolina chickadees and antshrikes, give an early warning of predators to the other members of the group.

Mammals can also be involved in these feeding associations. Birds and squirrels sometimes feed together, the birds catching insects disturbed by the rodents and providing an early warning of danger. In the tropics, hornbills associate with dwarf mongooses (see box above).

Different species often nest near each other to gain protection from predators. Gulls, terns, and waders sometimes nest in mixed colonies—the more pairs that nest together, the more vigilant and effective at defense the colony as a whole will be. Birds often nest on the fringes of nests of birds of prey: house sparrows near imperial eagles, African weavers near black kites, geese and waders with snowy owls. Water thick-knees, a kind of wading bird, place their nests near those of crocodiles. In this case, the bird acts as a sentinel, warning the crocodile of danger, while the crocodile keeps predators away from the bird's nest. Birds also often nest near colonies of wasps, bees, or ants—the insects sting any predators that encroach on the nest while the birds mob animals that eat insects.

▽ *Different species of birds often nest together, gaining protection from predators such as foxes and skuas due to their sheer numbers and from their proximity to each other. In Scotland, mallard ducks, gulls and oyster-catchers all nest within inches of each other.*

▷ *Crocodiles and hippos often visit well established "cleaning stations" operated by cleaner birds, which enter their hosts' mouths confidently, removing parasites and food scraps. Cleaner wrasses perform the same service for sharks—though false cleaner fish, which mimic the true cleaners' coloration, take advantage of their hosts when they can by darting in to seize a piece of fish.*

Cleaning services

Cleaning associations, with one species feeding on the parasites of another, are seen among various groups of animals. Some birds such as oxpeckers feed on the parasites of grazing mammals. Fish regularly come to fixed stations where they are attended to by cleaner fish and cleaner shrimps which remove parasites, diseased tissue, damaged scales, and pieces of uneaten food. The fish benefit greatly from the attentions of the cleaners. If the latter are removed, the fish either move out or succumb to disease. The cleaners in turn have a regular supply of food. The cleaners are small enough to be eaten by some of the fish they clean but they are hardly ever harmed.

▽ *Yellow- and red-billed oxpeckers live in close association with grazing animals such as wildebeest, gazelles, and zebras, not only cleaning parasites such as ticks from their hosts but swooping to snap up insects that are flushed from the grass as the hosts graze.*

Humans and animals

Humans are sometimes involved in close relationships with other species, often as hosts to parasites but also in some commensal and mutualistic situations. Swallows build their nests in our barns. Gulls follow our tractors to cash in on the worms turned up. One bird, the honeyguide, deliberately leads humans to the nests of bees which it cannot open itself. When the humans break open the nest, both they and the bird gain access to a rich source of food. Some cases of domestication of animals, such as dogs to hunt and guard the home, have also been to mutual advantage, providing the animals with food, shelter, and security from predators.

A fine line

There is sometimes a fine line between species being parasitic on and being beneficial to each other. The giant cowbird is a brood parasite, laying its eggs in nests of oropendolas and caciques (species of American blackbirds). The parasite chick takes food intended for the host, but in some circumstances its presence benefits its host. The chicks of the oropendolas and caciques suffer from botfly attacks—a heavy infestation can kill them. But the cowbird chick eats the botfly larvae and so helps the host chick. This benefit occurs only when the hosts are not nesting near wasp or bee nests because wasps and bees will also eat the deadly botflies. Caciques and oropendolas nesting near these insects also enjoy protection from predators such as opossums, toucans and snakes. But there is a down side: they have to have a shorter breeding season to fit in with the insects' own breeding activity, and the combined weight of the insects' and birds' nests often breaks the branch supporting them.

THE MANY RELATIONSHIPS OF ANTS

Ants form symbiotic relationships with many other creatures. Their large nests are a good source of shelter and food. Some ants guard aphids from predators and themselves feed on the honeydew, a byproduct of digestion, exuded by the aphids. The larvae of blue butterflies live protected within ants' nests, and in return they supply food by secreting a nutritious substance relished by their protectors.

Some inhabitants of ants' nests are commensals. Millipedes living in the nests of army ants scavenge food and gain some protection from predators without affecting the ants. Other insects spend all their lives as parasites within ants' nests. One beetle lives and breeds in ants' nests, both the adults and larvae inducing worker ants to regurgitate food for them, by copying the signals that the ants themselves use to beg for food from each other. Ants will regurgitate food if they are tapped lightly on the head, so they are easily duped. The beetles gain entrance to the ants' nests simply by approaching an ant and secreting appeasement substances which the ant finds attractive to eat; the duped ant then carries the beetle into its nest.

Mites ride on their ant hosts and either steal food when the ant regurgitates food for another ant, or persuade the ant to regurgitate food directly for them. One mite feeds on blood taken from the tip of the hind leg of its army ant host. When attached to the ant's leg it effectively becomes the ant's foot. Army ants cluster together when the group is at rest, one ant hooking the tip of its leg over another ant. If a mite is attached to the leg it becomes the hook instead.

Brood parasites occur among the social insects as well as among birds. But forcing other species to look after one's own offspring is taken to extremes in the slave-making ants. These raid the nests of other ants and carry the larvae and pupae back to their own nest—and when they mature these tend the slavers' larvae and even participate in further raiding parties.

◁ *There are almost as many strategies for survival with other organisms as there are varieties among Earth's thousands of species of ants, from the gardener ants that tend underground fungi to species that maintain "herds" of aphids, which they milk for honeydew.*

C

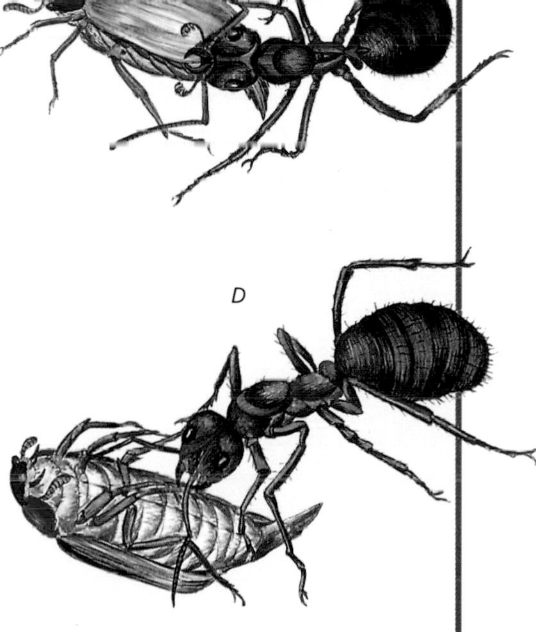

△ *A beetle gains entry to an ants' nest by secreting appeasement substances from glands that the ant licks (C) and then the beetle is carried into the nest by the ant (D) where it proceeds to live and breed, fed by the ants.*

A

△ *A tiny mite called* Macrocheles *attaches itself to the tip of the hind leg of its host, an army ant (A). Apparently content to serve as the ant's foot, it sucks body fluids from its host's body, also helping its host attach itself to other army ants when they form bivouacs (see page 67).*

B

◁ *Despite their migratory lifestyle, army ants attract a number of "camp followers," including a relatively large species of silverfish that spends most of its time riding on its host's body (B), which it cleans of smaller parasites and from which it scrapes and licks body secretions.*

INSTINCT AND INTELLIGENCE

SURVIVAL SKILLS

Dr. Raymond B. Huey

The world of an animal presents many challenges. Sometimes these challenges come from other animals, but often they come from the environment itself. A heat wave, a drought, or freezing rain may cause great suffering—even injury or death.

The ways animals have evolved to survive such extremes of climate are diverse and often elaborate, and include many behavioral and physiological strategies. The survival skills that enable an animal to survive a single cold night, however, may not be effective for an animal trying to survive the prolonged cold of a winter or of an ice age, so strategies depend not only on the type of stress an animal faces but also on its duration and severity.

One unifying theme underlying the diversity of animal survival skills is that behavioral adjustments alone are generally the most effective and universal ways of surviving stresses from nature. Merely by changing their behavior, animals can often evade or at least ameliorate stressful conditions in their world, whether of short or long duration.

What kinds of climates cause stress?
Heat, cold, drought, and flooding are obvious examples of environmental stresses. We humans are of course very sensitive to these particular climate stresses, and we often assume that such conditions—for example a heat wave in summer—will also cause animals to suffer. Conversely, we assume that conditions that are pleasant for us are also pleasant for animals. These assumptions are only sometimes true. Consider, for instance, a human family having a picnic in a high mountain meadow on a bright windless day in summer. We find such conditions ideal for picnics. But to a small butterfly exposed to the intense rays of the sun at high elevation, a bright

Above: Fur seals coming onshore to breed on the Pribilof Islands in Alaska experience very cold, wet, and overcast weather. But because these fur seals are so well insulated with fur and blubber, they would suffer from heat stress if they tried to breed somewhere less rigorous. Left: Wolves must use their cooperative hunting skills to bring down large animals such as deer. Their thick fur also helps them withstand the cold and survive when food is scarce.

△ ▽ *Reptiles in particular thrive in conditions that often induce stress in birds or mammals. Dry-country lizards, such as the common agama or dragon lizard (below), readily tolerate high body temperatures and considerable desiccation. Not all reptiles are so tolerant. Some tropical forest lizards, such as the anole (above), live in relatively benign environments and are much less tolerant of heat and desiccation.*

windless day poses a real threat. Without a wind to cool its body, it quickly overheats and could die within 10 minutes.

Animals differ strikingly from each other as well as from us in the range of conditions they can tolerate for survival. Temperatures that would be far too cold for a tropical fish will be far too warm for an Antarctic ice fish.

Mad dogs and Englishmen

High temperatures cause many problems for animals. If the animal's body temperature rises more than a few degrees, important physiological processes can be disrupted, and the animal can even die. Simply to stay cool, birds and mammals must evaporate large quantities of water by panting or sweating.

The most effective way to avoid the heat of the day is not to go out in it! Recall the old adage that "only mad dogs and Englishmen go out in the midday sun." In fact most animals avoid the heat of the day by staying in a cool retreat—in the shade of a tree, under a rock, or down a burrow.

The canyon lizard lives in the southwestern deserts of the United States and adjacent parts of Mexico. In the rocky canyons in which these lizards live, daytime rock temperatures regularly exceed 140°F (60°C)—hot enough to kill a desert lizard within a few minutes. In fact, virtually all of the ground surface during summer is above the lizard's lethal temperature from about 9.30 am to 6.30 pm. How do these lizards survive in such a hostile environment? Quite simply. In summer months they venture out onto the rocks only when temperatures aren't excessive—very early in the morning and again very late in the afternoon. They spend most of the day deep in a crevice, where temperatures are hot but tolerable.

Many desert rodents avoid heat stress by becoming active only at night. They spend the day down a cool burrow or in a hole in a tree trunk. Some desert snakes change their times of activity seasonally. In spring or fall they are active by day, but during the summer they come out only at night.

The extreme heat in the middle of the day in the Sahara Desert means that all animals—including all predators—avoid activity then. Well, almost all animals avoid activity then. Scientists recently discovered that the Saharan silver ant comes out of its underground nest only during the hottest time of day! By being active under conditions that are intolerable to predatory lizards in the area, this amazingly heat-tolerant ant seemingly benefits from being able to scavenge for food without risk of attack.

Even in a desert at midday, an animal may often find relief from the extreme heat under the shade of a tree, down a burrow, or at a cool water hole. But although shade offers protection from the sun, it may expose animals to other dangers. Some predators hide under shade trees, waiting for prey to come to them. Similarly, huge ticks in the Kalahari Desert of Africa swarm out of the leaf litter under acacia trees whenever antelopes or humans seek respite in the shade.

◁ Although they are commonly regarded as "cold-blooded," lizards and snakes such as this Cape cobra are actually highly efficient users of energy, with food requirements far below those of mammals. Moreover, venomous snakes like the Cape cobra are very efficient hunters, for their potent venom readily kills its bird and mammal prey.

Self- and Solar-powered Animals

The physiology of an organism affects the nature of stress. Birds and mammals are called "endotherms" because their main source of body heat comes from their own metabolic furnaces. Endothermy allows these animals to stay warm and active even under very cold conditions, but it comes at a severe energetic cost: the food requirements of a bird or mammal may be 30 to 50 times that of an equivalent-sized lizard or fish. Lizards, frogs, fishes, insects, and other invertebrates are called "ectotherms" because their main source of heat comes from the environment. These "solar-powered" animals require little food and water to survive, but they can be active only under a narrow range of environmental conditions.

When the environment becomes cool, ectotherms may become cool and sluggish, and they may be unable to digest their food.

△ ▷ Mammals can remain active under the most severe conditions, but do so only by consuming large amounts of food. A mouse risks literally starving to death unless it consumes a substantial percentage of its own body weight in food every day, whereas a similarly sized lizard, which has a lower "energy budget" because it relies in part on the sun's heat to provide it with energy, can survive for a week or more on a single meal.

Death Under the Sun

The giant tortoises that live on the Indian Ocean island of Aldabra tend to congregate near shade trees, and sometimes deplete nearby food resources. Driven by hunger, a few tortoises choose to leave the shade and migrate to other parts of the island, where food supplies are ample. The tortoises are fully exposed to the hot tropical sun during these journeys and risk overheating. Some areas of Aldabra are littered with the bleached shells of tortoises that died on the trek. Heat stress is particularly dangerous for eggs and young animals, which are usually far less tolerant of extremes of temperature than are mature adults. During a heat wave, many young will perish. The sand grouse of the Kalahari Desert in southern Africa has evolved a unique way to cool its eggs and young even on a blistering day in summer. These birds fly—sometimes many miles—to a waterhole. Their specialized belly feathers then soak up the water much like a sponge. The birds then fly back to the nest and use the water they have collected to cool their eggs or nestlings.

△ *Young animals are at greater risk of heat stress than adults. The sand grouse of the Kalahari shields its young from the worst of the sun's heat and provides them with water collected in its breast feathers.*

△ *Although ectothermy—the partial reliance on solar heat for energy that is characteristic of reptiles—has many advantages in a warm climate, it is not always reliable. Cool weather slows reptiles such as land iguanas dangerously, making them vulnerable to the Galapagos hawk ... which catches far more iguanas on cold days than during more normal warmer weather.*

Playing it cool

Cold conditions can be equally stressful to some animals. Low body temperatures slow the body processes of ectotherms, and under extremely cold conditions these animals may even freeze. Temperatures need not be freezing cold to be stressful, however, for the simple slowing of physiological processes at low temperature can create danger. A warm lizard is agile and can often outrun a predator, but a cold lizard is quite sluggish and potentially more vulnerable. In the Galapagos Islands, juvenile land iguanas are regularly caught and eaten by Galapagos hawks on cold days, but not on warm ones.

Because of the risks associated with activity during cold periods, many temperate-zone ectotherms head for a safe retreat and hibernate there quietly until spring. Many desert lizards and snakes bury themselves a few inches below the sand surface, and others crawl down a burrow or hide under a rock. By becoming inactive and allowing their body temperatures to drop during winter, hibernating ectotherms greatly reduce their requirements for food and water. More, their shelter protects them from the extremes of weather above ground and even from some predators.

From "flight" to "fight"

Some ectotherms do remain active in winter —in fact, a few specialized insects are active only in the colder months. Several insects can be found walking over the surface of glaciers in winter. Some desert lizards are active in winter only on relatively warm days. Rather than being active early and late in the day, as they are in summer, winter-active lizards restrict their activity to the middle of the day, when temperatures are highest, and they are almost always found fully exposed to the warming rays of the sun. So their habitat use and activity times change conspicuously between summer and winter.

When an anole lizard from Jamaica is cold, it becomes more wary and will retreat towards a shelter when an approaching predator is still distant. In contrast, a warm and agile anole will allow the predator to come much closer before the lizard retreats.

◁ ▽ Unique among terrestrial lizards, the marine iguanas of the Galapagos live on seaweed, which they obtain by diving into the cold Pacific. Unfortunately, algae digests very slowly, especially so if the iguana's body temperature is low. To help stay warm and thus speed digestion at night when basking in the sun is impossible, marine iguanas huddle overnight in large piles. Such social "cuddling" thus promotes the digestion rate of iguanas!

Several other lizards also switch their defensive behavior with temperature. When they are warm, two species of agamid lizards from the Middle East run at high speed from a predator, but when they are cold and sluggish the lizards stand upright, hold their ground, extend their throat fan, open their mouths, stick out their tongues, and even leap to bite. Thus, as body temperature drops, the lizards change their defensive behavior from "flight" to "fight." Presumably, this behavioral shift increases their chances of escaping predators.

Paper wasps have a parallel behavioral shift. On warm days, the wasps defend their nests by attacking and stinging a predator. On very cold days, however, the wasps can't fly. So they line up on the surface of the nest with their stingers pointing out from the nest. A predator would have to be hungry indeed to attack such a well defended nest!

Huddling and shivering

Cool temperatures can also cause internal physiological problems. The marine iguana of the Galapagos Islands eats algae, which it finds by diving into the cold Pacific Ocean. Algae is difficult to digest, and the iguanas must try to stay warm for as long as possible to process this food. During the day, the iguanas can readily stay warm merely by basking in the hot tropical sun. At night, however, they have difficulty staying warm. Most adults are too large to crawl under a warm rock. So, rather than let their temperatures drop, these large lizards form large lizard piles. By cuddling together they can stay warm for several hours, and can thus continue to digest their food.

In cold conditions, some insects have a remarkable ability to warm their bodies without basking. Many actively shiver their wing muscles, thereby generating enough heat to enable them

△ *For African dung beetles, bigger means warmer ... eventually. Large beetles take longer than small beetles to warm up enough to fly to freshly deposited dung, but they collect more dung in which to lay their eggs.*

to fly even on cold days—by doing this, some noctuid moths can fly with body temperatures near freezing, even on a day with air temperatures below freezing.

When an elephant or a large antelope defecates in the savannas of East Africa, the smell of the feces is rapidly carried downwind and attracts dung beetles. At night, however, the beetles are too cold to fly, and they must first shiver to warm. The bigger the beetle, the longer before it is warm enough to fly. When they finally reach a take-off temperature, they fly upwind to the dung, break off a ball of dung, roll it away for some distance, bury it underground, and then lay an egg on it. The resulting larval dung beetle feeds on the dung until it is big enough to metamorphosize into an adult. Because hundreds of beetles may be attracted to the same pile of dung, the competition for the dung can be intense. The winners of these fights are the biggest and the warmest beetles.

▽ *Although we tend to think of migration as a behavioral strategy for avoiding the cold of winter, some animals migrate to avoid the heat of summer. A small black flycatcher called a phainopepla, which lives in the southwestern deserts of the United States, spends the winter in the deserts. But as soon as the deserts start to get hot in summer, the birds move to cooler surrounding areas.*

Social endotherms often huddle together to stay warm in winter. Some species of birds crowd together on tree trunks on particularly cold nights, presumably reducing the surface area of their bodies exposed to the cold air.

Many mammals huddle in groups in response to cold. The degree of sociality changes seasonally in voles: during summer they are very intolerant of one another, but in winter they become tolerant, presumably to facilitate huddling.

Some mammals hibernate in groups: as many as 20 alpine marmots hibernate together for up to seven months in underground burrows in the Bavarian Alps. By huddling tightly with their offspring, parent marmots help keep themselves and their offspring warm during the long cold winter and greatly increase the chances that the offspring will survive until spring.

Warm bloods in the cold

During periods of prolonged cold, ectotherms allow their body temperatures to drop, but endotherms generally use their metabolic "furnaces" to stay warm, and may have a hard time doing so. If sleet is combined with cold temperatures, many may die.

Endotherms survive extreme cold in several very different ways. Many species simply migrate to warmer climates for the winter (see the Migration chapter, pages 123-131). A number of mammals and even some birds hibernate in winter (see box "Bulimic and Anorexic Mammals," opposite). Other species do remain active even in the cold of winter. But when temperatures drop, winter-active endotherms must produce much more body heat to stay warm—which means they must find more food to fuel their metabolic furnaces. They face severe problems in winter: days are short, and food resources on the ground may be covered with snow or ice. Winter-active birds may spend most and sometimes all of their daylight hours searching for food just to stay alive. Interestingly, these birds are noticeably less aggressive toward other birds on such cold days—they simply can't afford to spend their time fighting.

Bulimic and Anorexic Animals

Hibernators generally allow their body temperatures to drop well below normal levels during the winter months. As a result they greatly lower their metabolic rates, thus conserving fat and water. Because food is often difficult to obtain in winter, hibernation may be as much an adaptation for seasonal food shortages as for cold temperatures.

Most hibernators never allow their body temperature to drop to near freezing level, but the Arctic ground squirrel in Alaska allows its body temperature to drop to below freezing level. Studies of how these super-cooled squirrels survive such low temperatures may eventually help biomedical researchers develop new techniques for "cryosurgery," a technique in which human body temperatures are lowered before surgery.

Just before entering hibernation, most hibernators gorge on food and become quite fat. In fact, at the beginning of hibernation, about a quarter of the body mass of a golden-mantled ground squirrel is fat! During winter the squirrels may not feed at all. Thus, bulimia and anorexia are normal parts of the life cycles of these mammals. During the pre-hibernation feeding binge, some mammals not only eat more food but also change the types of food they eat. Some rodents appear to switch their preferences to foods that are high in unsaturated fats. Laboratory studies suggest that mammals fed diets high in unsaturated fats are able to hibernate at lower body temperatures, which should enable them to conserve energy during winter.

The red-backed vole of Europe is an exception to the rule of pre-winter fattening. These voles actually shrink just before winter. Apparently, by going on a diet and reducing their total body size, they reduce their food requirements. When spring arrives, these voles quickly begin to eat again and regain their weight.

△ *Surviving the harsh winters of the northern hemisphere generally means gorging on food during fall. Arctic ground squirrels double their body fat before going into hibernation.*

◁ *Some mammals take the opposite tack, actually losing weight before winter so that they have less mass to keep warm. The red-backed vole of northern Europe risks starvation during winter, but regains weight quickly in springtime.*

△ ▽ *Large mammals such as camels and elephants tolerate heat better than do smaller animals, primarily because large animals don't need to evaporate as much water per day simply to keep from overheating. Camels (above) have exceptionally low water requirements (about one-third that of a human). Their thick fur slows their rate of heat gain; and by allowing their body temperature to drop below normal at night and to increase above normal by day, camels save considerable water that otherwise would be required to keep them from overheating. Elephants (below) don't use these adaptations, but must drink at regular intervals. They are famous for their ability to remember the locations of scattered waterholes.*

▷ *(Above right) The thorny devil of arid Australia collects water—from rare showers or rain or dew—using a complex system of depressions and funnels between its "thorns" to channel moisture to its mouth.*

Conserving and replacing water

Free water is crucial for life. The bodies of most animals are 60 to 90 percent water, and animals require a regular supply of water to survive. So a drought represents a severe challenge. Small animals are especially vulnerable to desiccation, as they have very limited reservoirs of water in their bodies, but even large animals may suffer and even die during a severe drought.

Desiccation is also a danger to desert animals in summer. Hot dry air is very dehydrating. By simply breathing on hot days, an animal can lose large amounts of water. Desiccation can even be a problem at high elevation, as mountain climbers and plane travelers know all too well. Although air temperatures at high elevation are cool, water evaporates quickly in the thin air.

Despite their best efforts, animals can sometimes be exposed to hot, desiccating conditions. At such times, animals must cool their bodies by panting or by sweating. Unless the water that was evaporated is replaced, however, the animal may soon die of desiccation. Unfortunately, in the very same environments in which evaporative cooling is most effective, such as in deserts, replacement water is in short supply. So survival strategies for conserving and replacing water are well developed in desert animals. By spending the heat of the day underground, a beetle not only stays cool but simultaneously preserves its precious stores of body water. Similarly, by becoming active at night a desert rodent saves the water it would waste while panting to stay cool were it active by day.

Simply conserving water isn't enough to survive a prolonged drought, however. Animals must find new water to survive. Often, that water comes from their food—even dry seeds are a source of water, and many desert rodents such as the kangaroo rat and gerbil can survive summer purely on a diet of dry seeds.

Mobile animals such as birds and mammals sometimes move large distances to find water. The great migrations of wildebeest in East Africa follow the seasonal changes in rainfall. Elephants are renowned for their ability to recall the location of permanent waterholes, and they may travel long distances to reach them in a drought.

Some animals have evolved special ways to collect water. The Namib Desert, along the coast of southwestern Africa, provides several fascinating examples. Just offshore, the cold Benguela current sweeps north and creates a temperature inversion; little rain normally falls, but heavy fogs and dew at night are common. One species of tenebrionid beetle, normally active by day, crawls out to the crest of a sand dune on foggy nights, faces into the wind, and lifts its abdomen into the air. The fog droplets condense onto the beetle's body and trickle down to its mouth! A fog-drinking beetle can increase its body weight by 34 percent in one night. Another Namib beetle uses its body as a bulldozer and digs a trench perpendicular to the fog wind. As the fog moves across the dunes, it tends to condense on the small ridges of the trench. When the beetle retraces its steps, it licks the fog droplets from the sand! One sand-diving lacertid lizard also licks fog droplets from the Namib sand, and can store enough water to survive for many weeks.

Cicadas merely insert their long mouthparts through the bark of shrubs or trees and suck up plant juices as if they were at a drinking fountain. Because they have a ready supply of water always available, desert cicadas have the luxury of "wasting" water to stay cool by evaporation.

Dormant in the desert

During prolonged droughts, however, many animals aren't able to obtain adequate water supplies, and they may become dormant. To a casual observer, the land appears almost lifeless. Once the rains finally return, these long dormant animals suddenly come to life. Shortly after a cloudburst, desert frogs abruptly appear and start calling. Within a day, masses of small crustaceans such as fairy shrimps are teeming in temporary ponds. This sudden appearance of life after the breaking of a drought almost seems like a case of spontaneous generation.

How can these animals survive the long dormancy of a drought? After all, the skin of frogs is very permeable to water. In fact, a frog and a wet sponge lose water at about the same rate! So the mere existence of frogs in a desert is surprising. Desert frogs survive by spending most of their lives buried underground. Some even secrete several layers of skin, enveloping their entire body except for their nostrils. Inside these almost watertight "cocoons" the frogs rest quietly and very patiently. If and when the rains finally come, these frogs dig their way to the surface and begin to hunt for food and mates.

Fairy shrimps and other small crustaceans also spend the long periods between rains dormant in the clay. Rather than being dormant as adults, however, these crustaceans are typically dormant as eggs, which are extraordinarily tolerant of heat and desiccation. Eggs of tadpole shrimp can apparently tolerate 208°F (98°C) for up to 16 hours! When the rains come, the eggs quickly hatch and the shrimps grow rapidly to maturity, mate, and release their eggs—all, hopefully, before the pond again dries.

Life and death after rain

For many animals, the flush of life following a rain provides an abundance of food and water. Winged termites, which swarm in huge masses after a desert rain, are the favored food of many animals. In Africa these termites are devoured by many species of other insects, lizards, frogs, birds, and even mammals. Geckos, a group of nocturnal lizards, can stuff themselves with enough swarming termites in a single evening to survive for several months without another meal.

Although deserts are defined as areas of little rain, they are sometimes places of too much rain. A sudden cloudburst in summer can trigger a flash flood that inundates large areas, and frog tadpoles developing in a small pond can be swept away and killed in a raging muddy torrent. Underground ant colonies can be flooded beyond hope. For many animals in the direct path of a flash flood, survival is highly improbable.

Even animals that aren't actually trapped in a flood may suffer from the heavy rains. The huge nests of the sociable weaverbirds in Africa can become so heavy with water that they snap the branches that support them. The nest crashes to the ground, killing many birds. Similarly, the eggs of lizards incubating underground may not hatch in soils that are cool and wet.

Ironically, the flooding that kills many desert animals makes those same deserts suddenly inhabitable to many birds. During summers of exceptionally heavy rains, white storks, hamerkops, and African jacanas can be found walking over the red sand dunes of the Kalahari Desert. Presumably they find food in abundance then; but in a normal, dry year, these birds could never survive in such a place.

△ *Desert animals such as tadpole shrimps or fairy shrimps are amazingly tolerant of heat and dryness. Their eggs, covered by a horny membrane that will only soften after prolonged exposure to water, lie dormant for months or even years until rain falls, when in a few days they hatch, grow to adulthood, breed and die.*

▽ *Some desert animals can make their own shade. Antelope ground squirrels in the hot deserts of the American southwest and Cape ground squirrels (below) of the southern African deserts have fluffy tails. When temperatures begin to get hot in the morning, the squirrels lift their tails and shield themselves from the searing sun with their portable parasols. When temperatures finally drop in late afternoon, they drop their tails.*

MIGRATION

Professor Dr. Peter Berthold

Among the many million species in the animal kingdom, several hundred billion individuals are on the move at any one time, performing some kind of migration—usually, but by no means always, annual. These journeys are undertaken by all types of vertebrates, including fish, amphibians, reptiles, birds, mammals, and even man, and by many invertebrates, including butterflies, locusts, and marine crustaceans. Why do they all move? Ultimately, all types of migratory movements are somehow related to food—or lack of it.

Many of these journeys provide us with spectacles rarely, if ever, matched in nature. Many are also of quite staggering length and difficulty, involving nonstop flights over seas, mountains, and deserts for birds, or dangerous river crossings for mammals.

Animals on the move

Most of the animals considered typical migrants move horizontally on the earth's surface, often commuting between breeding areas and winter quarters. Amphibians such as frogs, that are ill-equipped for travel on land, normally migrate short distances to breed in a certain body of water. Some snakes can cover up to 9 miles (15 km) on their way to communal wintering spots. Other groups of migrants cover vast distances: marine crustaceans such as spiny lobsters walk on the bottom of the ocean for several hundred miles; the green sea turtle swims up to 2,000 miles (3,000 km) to lay its eggs; wandering desert locusts and North American monarch butterflies migrate over distances of 2,500 miles (4,000 km). Records for fish are held by sockeye salmon (2,000–2,300 miles, or 3,000–3,500 km). Land-living mammals are not great travelers: the record is held by the wildebeest of Africa, which travels about 600 miles (1,000 km). But marine mammals such as the northern fur seal and the humpback whale cover 3,000 to 4,000 miles (5,000 to 7,000 km).

Animal migration is inspired by the search for food or by the need, in the case of some fishes and marine invertebrates, to return to spawning grounds. The prodigious distances involved, from the wildebeest's 600-mile (1,000 km) trek across the African plains (left) to the monarch butterfly's 2500-mile (4,000 km) journey (above), have long been a source of fascination.

△ *Rüppell's griffon vultures can fly at heights of 35,000 feet (10,500 m), where the atmospheric pressure is only a fifth of that at sea level.*

THE MILLION-MILERS

Arctic terns travel from their Arctic breeding grounds in North America, Greenland, or Siberia to their winter quarters in Antarctic waters every year without fail. There is good evidence that parts of the wintering community in addition circle the Antarctic continent before returning.

Thus these terns cover between 18,000 and 30,000 miles (30,000 and 50,000 km) per year—roughly the same distance as the entire circumference of the earth. As a substantial number of Arctic terns probably reach a life expectancy of approximately 25 years, those birds could theoretically attain a lifetime migratory mileage of over a million miles.

▽ *Arctic terns navigate from the North Pole to the South every year, with some populations circling Antarctica before setting off on their return journey. Pausing only briefly to rest on the waves, these pigeon-sized birds circumnavigate the earth every year on their way to and from their northern nesting grounds.*

To the ends of the earth

By far the most formidable migratory performances are made by the most mobile group of vertebrates—the birds. They are in many ways adapted for rapid, long-distance, and even high-altitude migration, and they have consequently evolved a worldwide network of migratory routes. About half of the 9,000–odd species that currently exist annually perform some type of migratory movement—movement which involves roughly 50 thousand million individual birds.

Birds cover the globe. They use almost every conceivable area for breeding, including the most remote corners of the earth. Birds are capable of successfully crossing deserts like the Sahara, mountains like the Himalayas, and all oceans and extended icefields. The records for distances, nonstop flights, flight times and altitude are very striking.

Birds often have to cross oceans, inhospitable deserts, mountains, and icefields on extended nonstop flights. Waders from Alaska or northeastern Siberia such as the golden plover, the bristle-thighed curlew, or the great knot are known to fly nonstop up to the Hawaiian islands or down to New Zealand. These nonstop flights range from 2,500 to 4,000 miles (4,000 to 7,500 km) and take an estimated 80 to 100 hours.

Small songbirds are also commonly forced to cross inhospitable areas like the Gulf of Mexico, the Sahara Desert, or the Atlantic or Pacific oceans during nonstop flights of more than 600 miles (1,000 km), flights which take them about 30 hours. And even a real dwarf among birds, the ruby-throated hummingbird, which has a body mass of just about one sixth of an ounce (5 grams), is capable of crossing the Gulf of Mexico nonstop.

In the Himalaya region, birds migrating from Siberia to wintering areas on the Indian subcontinent cross the world's highest mountains. Sight recordings range up to 27,000 feet (9,500 m). Radar studies of migratory birds have shown that birds can reach similar altitudes in other areas as well. The world's record holder is presently a Rüppell's griffon, which ran into an aircraft over the Ivory Coast in Africa at an altitude of 35,000 feet (11,300 m).

◁ *The Arctic tern undertakes a longer migration than any other bird. Each year it flies from its winter quarters in Antarctica to breed in the Arctic, and then back again, a round trip of more than 30,000 kilometers. Such behavior means that it spends almost all of its life in long daylight hours, affording it plenty of time to feed.*

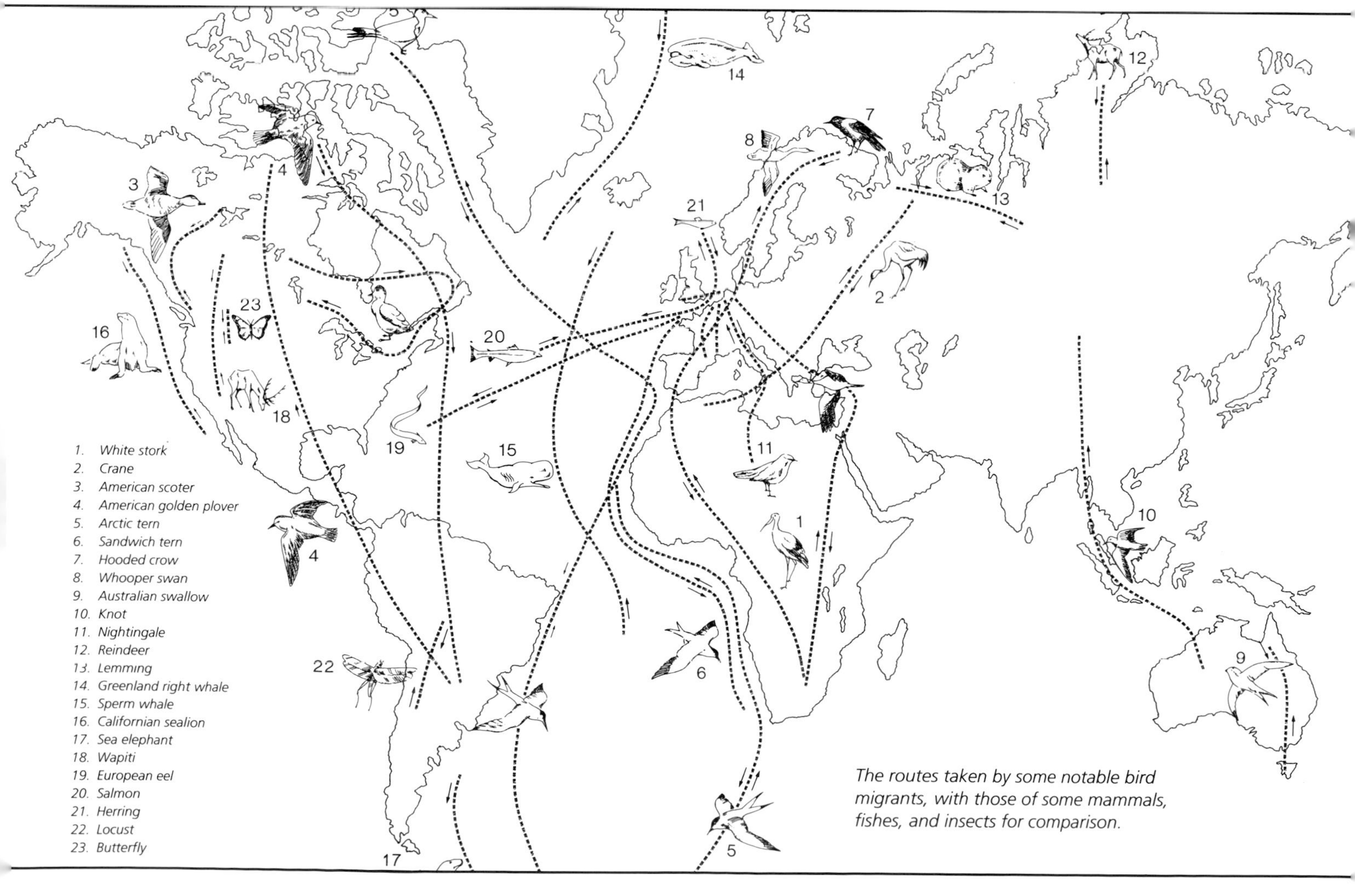

1. *White stork*
2. *Crane*
3. *American scoter*
4. *American golden plover*
5. *Arctic tern*
6. *Sandwich tern*
7. *Hooded crow*
8. *Whooper swan*
9. *Australian swallow*
10. *Knot*
11. *Nightingale*
12. *Reindeer*
13. *Lemming*
14. *Greenland right whale*
15. *Sperm whale*
16. *Californian sealion*
17. *Sea elephant*
18. *Wapiti*
19. *European eel*
20. *Salmon*
21. *Herring*
22. *Locust*
23. *Butterfly*

The routes taken by some notable bird migrants, with those of some mammals, fishes, and insects for comparison.

△ Like chamois, red deer migrate vertically in response to the availability of food. In late spring and summer they move up into the mountains to feed on summer grasses in alpine meadows; in fall they retreat downward to shelter in thick forest (where their fawns are also born), since they cannot break through thick snow to graze.

The migratory urge

Many of these animal feats are almost unbelievable to us. How can a tiny creature like a butterfly accomplish a 2,500 mile (4,000 km) journey, or a hummingbird a nonstop flight of 600 miles (1,000 km)? How can migratory animals keep on schedule on journeys as long as 18,000 miles (30,000 km)? And what tells them when to leave an area in order to arrive at their goal at the appropriate time?

Scientists have discovered the answers to most of the how, why, where, and when questions of migration during the past 30 years. In some cases they are rather simple. For instance, mountain-living species such as deer or Alpine choughs go through a short-range vertical migration to the next suitable lowland in response to snow cover. They may stay in the mountains during years without heavy snow cover, or they may go back before the winter ends when the snow melts in a mild period. These animals are clearly triggered by climatic factors such as snow and the associated food shortage, and can sense favorable or unfavorable conditions within their adjacent breeding and wintering areas.

But what about long distance migrants? What about, for instance, most of the temperate-zone insectivorous songbirds, which often leave during the peak of the summer to winter in the tropics? What tells them when to take off from the breeding grounds or when to leave tropical wintering areas to return northward or southward? And what brings them within the same few days to remote breeding areas year after year?

Twenty years ago, physiologists discovered that migratory birds, like hibernating mammals, are equipped with innate calendars. These biological clocks produce annual physiological and behavioral rhythms as other biological clocks do in the form of daily rhythms. Migratory birds raised and kept in constant experimental conditions, where the normal seasonal changes in environmental factors such as day length, temperature, and food supply are kept constant, still show annual rhythms in reproduction, feather molt, and migration.

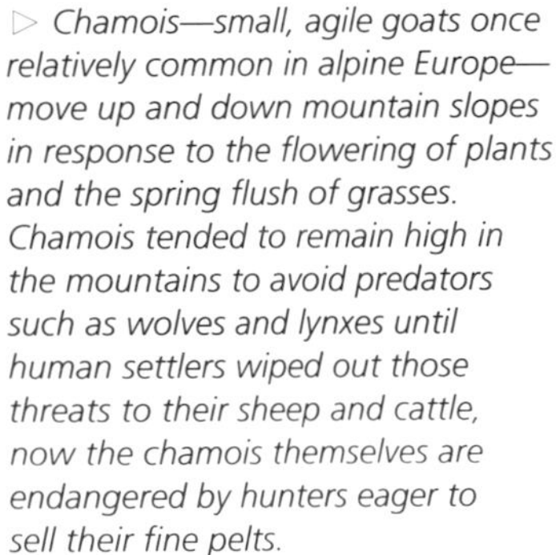

▷ Chamois—small, agile goats once relatively common in alpine Europe—move up and down mountain slopes in response to the flowering of plants and the spring flush of grasses. Chamois tended to remain high in the mountains to avoid predators such as wolves and lynxes until human settlers wiped out those threats to their sheep and cattle, now the chamois themselves are endangered by hunters eager to sell their fine pelts.

▷ (Far right) Monarch butterflies migrate up into the mountains to escape the lowland heat of summer.

△ *Ironically, it took scientists decades to realize that the central mystery of animal navigation had already been solved by human sailors. The sea is devoid of landmarks, and that the only way to navigate through such trackless wastes is to follow the sun and the stars—as migrating green turtles do.*

The migratory urge is expressed in specific hormonal and metabolic states. It is most obvious in the body mass increase: the deposition of fat as a "fuel load" before migration. It also manifests itself in the restlessness displayed by nocturnal migratory birds such as warblers, thrushes, and waders; in captivity they whirr their wings and hop about as the time for migrating approaches.

The internal calendar also provides innate time programs for the journey. Many studies, including cross-breeding experiments with short- and long-distance migrating birds and mammals, have shown that individuals are programmed to express migratory activity for a set amount of days, weeks, or months, for whatever time is necessary to cover the distance between the breeding and the wintering areas. In combination with innate migratory directions, migrating birds ot mammals can possess heritable programs which enable inexperienced individuals to "automatically" get to their unknown winter quarters.

The functions of fat

Migratory fat deposition has four main functions. First, fat provides, as a rule, the fuel for the entire migration. Next, the use of fat during migratory journeys produces a considerable amount of metabolic water (slightly more than 1 gram per gram of fat burned) that plays an important role in water balance during flights across deserts and other areas where drinking water is scarce. Thus fat metabolism during migration provides migrants with an internal water supply. Fat deposition also increases body mass and this, due to flight mechanism properties, generally leads to higher flight speeds in birds. Finally, fat deposits are often still considerable even after migrants have reached their breeding grounds. This is quite pronounced in early arrivals, who reach the grounds when living conditions are still poor or unstable. Fat reserves thus provide safety margins for the survival of migratory animals.

Not surprisingly, therefore, almost all migratory animals are preprogrammed to

◁ *Following chemical cues too subtle for humans to detect, salmon are capable of migrating across thousands of miles of ocean to the very streams where they hatched. They cease to eat when they enter fresh water, relying on reserves of fat to complete the arduous journey upstream and lay their own eggs.*

▽ *Although wildebeest migrate only across some 600 miles (1,000 km), they face many hardships on their journey, from land predators such as lions and hyenas to river-dwelling predators such as crocodiles. If the wildebeest are to survive, they must gather abundant reserves of energy before they set out.*

develop migratory fat deposits. Their extent and development is amazing. Many long-distance migrating songbirds and waders double their body mass with enormous subcutaneous fat deposits, or layers of fat between and within their organs. Such birds often appear as if they were dressed in bacon.

The main mechanism for fattening is simply hyperphagia—in other words, overeating. But other factors are involved. For instance, the seasonal shift in many insectivorous songbirds in summer to eating berries and other pulpy fruits is very important. This dietary change provides both easy prey and large amounts of carbohydrates to promote fat production.

With this in mind, you may look more favorably on warblers or robins when next they come to your garden to consume some of the berries. The berries may be a necessary prerequisite for the birds to get back safely from their migratory journey next spring and entertain you again with their song.

A Sense of Location

Dr. R. Robin Baker

△ *A nestling bird born in the southern hemisphere learns to orient itself by observing the rotation of the stars in the night sky around the South celestial pole. However, we still do not know how those species that migrate from one hemisphere to another and back again learn how to adjust their internal "compasses" so they can find their way through unfamiliar skies.*

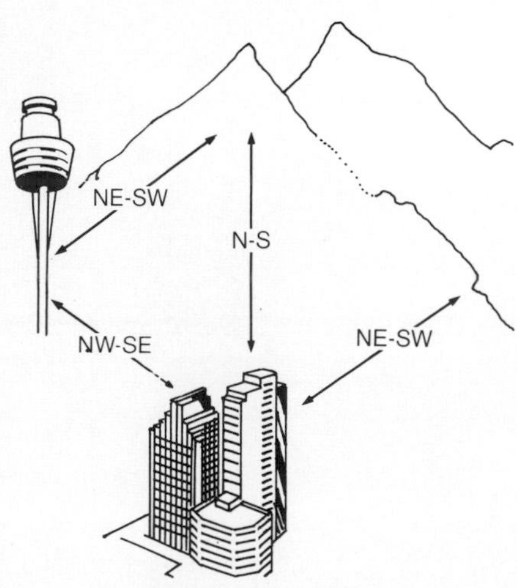

△ *The spatial relationships of major landmarks are memorized in terms of their relative compass bearings.*

A sense of location allows us to organize our life and movements with great efficiency. Our daily movements consist of a series of return migrations—to places to work, sleep, eat and drink, and so on—with only occasional breaks from the pattern during an entire lifetime. Most of the time, we know where we are, where we are going, and where we could go to get just about anything we want. We are able to do this because we carry around in our head a mental map that contains all the information we need, and this mental map gives us our sense of location.

It would be surprising if humans were the only species to have evolved such a sense. It is much more likely that we inherited this ability from our prehuman ancestors. And indeed, it turns out that other animals, including primates, have a highly sophisticated sense of location. The more that is discovered about the sense of location of humans and other animals, the more difficult it becomes to see any real difference between them.

Developing a mental map

As humans, we are used to the idea that we find new places to eat, drink, or even live by occasional exploratory forays into unfamiliar terrain. We now know that all animals with a sense of location rely heavily on such exploration to build up their familiar area and develop their mental map.

Young rabbits, before they are old enough to reproduce, set off on twilight explorations after their evening feed. They travel at a steady lope, often pausing to stand on their hind legs, look around, and sniff the evening air. Eventually, they settle down in one of the many places they first visited during this adolescent exploration.

The homing experiments by which scientists study an animal's sense of direction in effect simply mimic exploration. Animals are taken from their homes and forced to visit a new, previously unfamiliar location. They are then tested for their ability to set off in the direction of home. Such experiments usually limit the range of environmental clues some of the animals can perceive and then compare the performance of these animals with the performance of the untreated control animals.

In this way, homing experiments have allowed the mechanisms underlying the sense of location of different animals to be studied. The surprising conclusion is that, whether the animal being studied is a bee, bird, or human, the navigational techniques used are very similar.

Most is known about birds. The mental map carried around in the head of a bird does not contain detailed information about the bird's entire familiar area. Instead, the map is a mosaic of important sites, each identified by memorized landmarks and the compass bearings of that site in relation to other such sites. Such a mosaic format is very economical for a mental map. Not only is it efficient for local movements, it permits travel over huge distances via the memorization of large-scale geographical features, such as oceans and mountain ranges, and of the compass directions that link them. Mosaic maps allow birds to travel thousands of miles over the earth during seasonal migration without the need to memorize impossible amounts of information.

Navigating by the sun and stars

Much is known about the environmental clues used by birds to identify landmarks and compass directions in the formation of their mental maps. As far as landmarks are concerned, birds undoubtedly note and memorize visible geographical features. They also memorize familiar smells and perhaps even familiar sounds. Birds can detect infrasounds, those very long wavelength sounds which go undetected by the human ear but which are given off by air currents passing over mountain ranges and shorelines and even just by thunderstorms. This ability to detect infrasound could allow them to "hear" landmarks such as mountain ranges and shorelines from distances of 600 miles (1,000 km) or more. In locating distant smells, birds are able to take into account the compass direction of the wind.

Birds use several environmental clues to gauge compass directions. First, like all animals properly studied so far, birds are born with the ability to discriminate compass directions using magnetoreception (that is, perception of the earth's magnetic field). The site of the sense organ which detects the magnetic field remains undiscovered. The two favorite theories are that the magnetic sense depends on either magnetic particles in the walls of the nostrils, and/or on large molecules in the retina of the eye which, when broken down, resonate in a particular way, depending on the direction of the magnetic field.

Birds are also born with a predisposition during their first few weeks of life to observe the rotation of the night sky and to locate the sky's axis of rotation (the hub around which the whole sky appears to rotate). This axis marks the direction of geographical north or south, depending on hemisphere; in the northern hemisphere it is marked by the Pole star. Having observed the rotating sky, the young bird learns how to locate the axis of rotation from the pattern of nearby stars.

△ *Following chemical cues at concentrations of only a few molecules per cubic foot of water, salmon can recognize the distinctive odors of the streams in which they hatched. However, the method by which they cross the open ocean and locate the mouths of those streams is still unknown.*

Finally, birds use their ability to judge direction from the magnetic field to learn the movement pattern of the sun across the sky during the day. Thereafter, they are able to use the sun as a compass, compensating with great accuracy for its apparent movement across the sky during the day.

As a bird, or any other animal, explores, it monitors the direction in which it is traveling by some combination of its ability to perceive distant landmarks and its sense of compass direction. By this means, when the animal discovers a potentially useful new site, it is already aware of the direction of home. Adding this new site to the familiar area is then simply a matter of committing the surrounding landmarks and the home compass bearing to memory on the mental map. Young birds, with still only a small familiar area, rely on following their outward journey with great accuracy in order to return to their tiny target. More experienced older birds with a larger familiar area seem to monitor their outward journey less accurately.

ADAPTING TO A CHANGING WORLD

Professor Tim Halliday

The concepts of adaptation and change are at the very heart of the theory of evolution by natural selection. Animals and plants change in their morphology, their physiology, and in their behavior over the course of evolutionary time because they are constantly adapting to new challenges presented by a changing environment. Some changes operate in the short term. An unusually harsh winter or a summer drought, an outbreak of disease, an environmental catastrophe such as a volcanic eruption; all provide immediate threats to the continued existence of a species, and it must adapt if it is to survive.

On a longer time scale, new species, of predators, parasites, and competitors, are constantly evolving; existing species must adapt or face extinction. Behind such changes are extremely slow, gradual changes as the earth's climate fluctuates and goes through a series of ice ages. Underlying that, the earth is slowly cooling down and the Sun is burning up. Animals and plants must adapt to such changes or become extinct. In the words of the Red Queen in Lewis Carroll's *Through the Looking Glass*, "Now here, you see, it takes all the running you can do, to keep in the same place."

Tolerating pollution

So slow is the process of evolution by natural selection that the way it works, and the course it has taken, have normally to be inferred from indirect evidence, such as by comparing living species, with one another and with fossils. There are, however, numerous examples of species that have undergone observable evolutionary change during human history. A number of insects, notably the peppered moth, have evolved dark, melanic forms that are adapted to be camouflaged on the blackened

The very concept of a wild animal is necessarily a human one, and has its origins in our own gradual separation from nature and move toward mechanization. Such distinctions are meaningless to animals such as these foxes (left) and hedgehogs (above), which are superbly adaptable to new conditions, whether these are the products of natural forces or human invention.

△ *The processes of adaptation and evolution favor opportunistic species that can adopt new ways of life in order to survive. Pigeons have adapted well to cities; likewise, European chaffinches (above) have prospered through their association with farms and hedgerows.*

trunks of trees in polluted areas of Britain. Many plants that grow on roadsides have evolved tolerance to the salt that is spread on roads in winter, and many others growing near mines have evolved tolerance to lead and other heavy metals. Insects such as mosquitoes that could previously be controlled by DDT and other insecticides have evolved resistance to their effects.

Animal opportunists

In the context of behavior, there are also examples of adaptive changes by animals, particularly to the presence and activities of humans. Rats, starlings, pigeons, and gulls have all increased enormously in numbers because they have incorporated human refuse into their diet. Many birds, such as pigeons, kittiwakes, and even birds of prey, commonly nest on buildings. For some animals, such as swifts and bats, buildings provide the most important sites for nesting and roosting. Many birds follow plows and ships while feeding, and kestrels hover beside roads looking for small animals that are killed or disturbed by traffic. Nocturnal animals such as geckos and toads gain rich pickings by sitting under or near lights and eating insects that fly into them. In Britain, huge quantities of bird food are sold every winter, to be left out on bird tables in cold weather. It is thought that this supplementation of their natural food has had a major positive impact on the populations of some species which otherwise suffer high mortality in winter.

Different kinds of adaptation

To say that a particular pattern of behavior is "adaptive" means that it enhances an individual animal's ability to survive, to reproduce, or both. Adaptive changes in behavior arise in three ways, acting on very different time scales and brought about by very different processes.

First, individual animals can learn; that is, they change their behavior in adaptive ways as a result of their experience. Hedgehogs and many birds can be trained to come to a garden for food, for example.

Second, individual animals can learn from one another so that an adaptive pattern of behavior can spread through a population as one animal copies another. This kind of process, which can lead to populations of a species living in different localities showing very different patterns of behavior, is called cultural transmission or cultural evolution. A striking example is provided by bird song. Many male birds

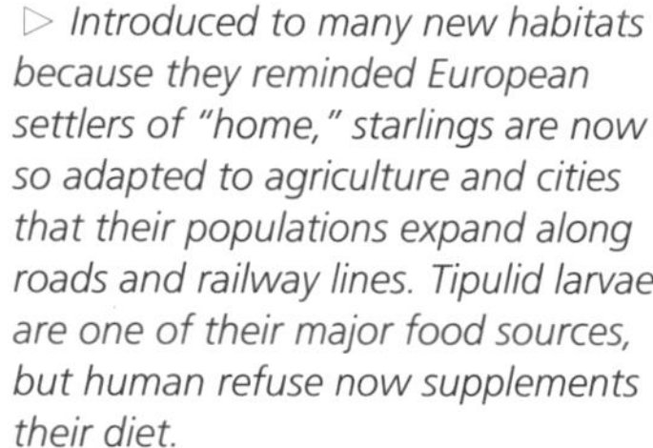

▷ *Introduced to many new habitats because they reminded European settlers of "home," starlings are now so adapted to agriculture and cities that their populations expand along roads and railway lines. Tipulid larvae are one of their major food sources, but human refuse now supplements their diet.*

learn the characteristic song of their species by listening to their father, and sometimes to other adult males. They do not imitate the song exactly, however, but make slight "errors," and they may incorporate snatches of song that they have heard sung by a number of males. As a result, many species have "local dialects," so that the song of a chaffinch, for example, is rather different in the south of England as compared with Scotland.

Finally, there is slow, evolutionary change, brought about by natural selection and affecting all members of a species exposed to that aspect of the environment that favors the adaptive change.

Adapting by learning

Learning refers to the ability of animals to alter their behavior in the light of their experience. An important category of learning is called associative learning, in which an animals makes an association between two stimuli. For example, birds will quickly learn to come for food at a bird table. They do this by associating one stimulus, the presence of food, with another, which might be the bird table itself, the time of day at which food is put out, or the sight or sound of the person who puts the food out. Detailed studies of kestrels have revealed that, when an individual finds a prey item such as a vole, it returns to that place, at the same time of day, for several days. As a result, kestrels patrol their home ranges in a regular pattern so that they come to particularly good feeding areas at times when food is most likely to be available there. Herring gulls living in a large colony in northern England that is very close to a large refuse tip have learnt when best to visit the tip so as to be there when refuse lorries are unloading, and they do not visit the tip at weekends.

For animals in the wild, it is important to learn about predators. If they are attacked by a predator and survive the experience, they will typically be more wary of it in the future. But such opportunities are rare, and many animals are killed before they can learn anything about their enemies. There is evidence, however, that animals seek out opportunities to learn about predators. Gulls, for example, gather in a flock around a fox or stoat as it eats one of their number, and many animals show intense interest in one of their fellows that has been killed. Small birds also mob predators much larger than themselves, such as birds of prey, gathering in a flock and attacking them. Mobbing serves several functions, most obviously driving the predator away; less obviously, it alerts other birds to the presence of the predator, and it provides an opportunity for individuals to learn what the predator looks like and how it behaves.

△ ▽ *The ability to learn about new factors in the environment is essential to survival; the faster and more complete the learning process, the greater the chances of profiting from the experience. Some animals, such as foxes (above) and hedgehogs (below) are especially willing to experiment with new food sources and have become common urban scavengers.*

HAMMERERS AND STABBERS

Individuals in many animal species have to learn how to find and handle their food. Because many animals can eat a variety of foods, and because the distribution of food types varies from place to place, it is often observed that different individuals within a population have very different diets. In a colony of herring gulls, for example, there are mussel specialists whose diet consists primarily of mussels, while others specialize on starfish or crabs. In the oystercatcher, individuals not only specialize on one type of food but also have different techniques for handling those foods. Oystercatchers feed largely on shellfish such as mussels, and have to extract the edible flesh from inside the shell. Some are hammerers: they remove a mussel from its rock and then hammer very hard with their sturdy beak at the weakest point in the shell to create a hole. Others are stabbers: they seek out mussels that are under water and whose shells are open, and very quickly stab their beak into the opening to cut the muscle that holds the two halves of the mussel shell together. Young birds learn their particular feeding technique—either stabbing or hammering—from their parents.

△ *Although many animals have anatomical adaptations to a specialized diet—for example, oystercatchers have strong, pointed beaks for penetrating and twisting open bivalve shells—they are not limited to a single feeding technique. Some hammer on a weak point to open a mussel, while others stab their beaks into oysters that are open underwater; behavior that oystercatcher chicks learn from their parents.*

▽ *Intelligent animals, such as rats, not only learn new behavior quickly, but pass information on to others. Information can be of immediate benefit to the population (for example, the location of a new source of food).*

Adapting by cultural transmission

Learning from other animals provides the basis of cultural evolution, in which behavior patterns spread through a population by animals imitating or copying one another. A well-known example is the spread across Britain of the habit that blue tits have of pecking through the foil tops of milk bottles left on doorsteps and helping themselves to the cream. This habit was observed to spread slowly from one part of Britain to another over several years. Recently, the habit has apparently largely died out, probably because many people now buy milk with a reduced cream content.

A very well-documented example of the cultural transmission of behavior is provided by food preparation behavior in the Japanese macaque. A group was being studied beside a large lake. So that the scientists could observe the behavior of the monkeys more easily, they left out sweet potatoes where the monkeys were most visible. After a while, a particular macaque, a 16-month-old female known as Imo, was seen to be taking her potatoes to a nearby stream to wash the dirt off them. This habit was gradually copied by other monkeys, particularly those in Imo's age group. Within 10 years, potato-washing had spread through the whole population, except to very young animals, less than one year old, and those over 12 years of age. Other new habits also appeared and spread through the group. One monkey invented the trick of separating rice from sand by dipping handfuls of the mixture into the water so that the rice floated and the sand sank.

A biologist observing such a group now might conclude that a widespread behavior pattern such as potato-washing must be a genetically determined part of the species' behavioral repertoire. It is only because the origins of the behavior were observed that we know that it is culturally rather than genetically determined.

Cultural transmission typically follows particular routes through a population. Young animals generally learn new behavior patterns more readily than older ones, and animals are more likely to copy the behavior of dominant, rather than subordinate individuals. Thus the age and status of the animal that invents a new behavior pattern affects the speed with which it is copied and adopted by others.

The fact that animals learn from one another has important implications for attempts by people to control certain species that are classed as pests by man. An attempt to reduce the numbers of the carrion crow using poisoned food failed because, after a few deaths, the rest of a flock would avoid the poisoned food.

Rats spend a great deal of time sniffing one another and can detect, by smell, the kind of food eaten recently by other members of their social group. If a group mate is obviously healthy, the other rats will then eat the food that it has eaten. If it is unwell, however, they will avoid the food it has been eating recently. A rat encountering a new food for the first time will sometimes urinate on it if it is distasteful, and so warns others to avoid it.

△ Blue tits are enthusiastic exploiters of new food supplies, especially in winter. Europeans first regarded tits' ability to open milk-bottles as an endearing and impressive example of adaptation; now, however, this ability is seen as merely irritating, and humans are utilizing their own adaptability in an effort to design bird-proof bottle tops.

◁ Exploiting human food sources has been added to the already wide range of behaviors shown by opportunistic species. Herring gulls fly inland to take advantage of insect swarms, whether in uninhabited country or on farms; resident gull populations at refuse dumps also fly out to sea to take advantage of schooling fish.

△ ▽ Companion animals such as cats first associated with humans because human habitations attracted other opportunistic species, such as rats—species we regard as pests because they exploit our resources. Gradually, cats' economic value was overridden by the pleasure they gave as pets, and the process of selection has been accelerated to produce new varieties. Rats have survived human's attempts at eradication through the use of poison due, in part, to their caution when approaching potential food.

Evolutionary changes

By their very nature, evolutionary changes resulting from natural selection take place over very long periods of time and are thus much less readily detected than changes due to learning or cultural transmission. Comparable changes are, however, very familiar to us in a wide range of domesticated species, whose appearance and behavior have been altered by artificial selection. Different breeds of dogs have been selected by people for their ability to go down fox holes, to retrieve shot game birds, to run very fast, or to guard their owners; different breeds of horses have been selected to race and to pull carts. A huge variety of purely decorative breeds have been developed in pigeons, aquarium fish, dogs, and cats. This kind of selection, which mimics natural selection, has involved conscious efforts by humans to produce animals with particular characteristics, but humans have also unconsciously created new selection pressures. For example, there are strains of mice living in cold stores that have evolved especially thick fur.

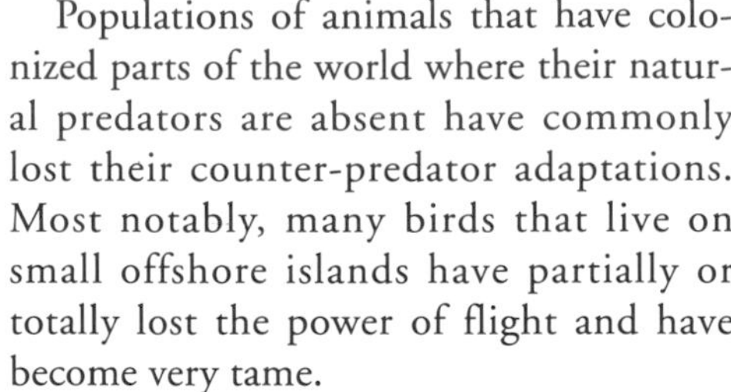

Populations of animals that have colonized parts of the world where their natural predators are absent have commonly lost their counter-predator adaptations. Most notably, many birds that live on small offshore islands have partially or totally lost the power of flight and have become very tame.

Geographical variation in anti-predator adaptations has been described in the three-spined stickleback. In parts of Europe where predators are abundant, sticklebacks have very large spines on their back and large armored plates on their flanks; they are also very wary of any large fish. By contrast, where predators are few, they have fewer and smaller spines, poorly developed armor, and are very bold in the presence of large fish. On the island of South Uist, off the west coast of Scotland, there are very few predatory fish and sticklebacks bely their name by being virtually spineless, and they show virtually no fear of larger fish.

Studies of local variation in appearance and behavior provide clear evidence that animals can adapt to local conditions as a result of natural selection. Examples such as male coloration in the guppy (see box "Protection or Mates?" on page 139) provide some of the most compelling evidence available for the process of natural selection. They also show very clearly how animals can adapt to changes in their immediate environment.

Facing the future

The ability of animals to adapt to a changing world means that some at least can adapt to the many and varied changes that humans have brought about in the natural environment. In Britain, for example, there has been a remarkable change in recent years in the behavior of the common fox. In a large number of towns and cities, foxes have become "urbanized," so that they now live and breed in the heart of large urban areas. They patrol the streets, feed out of garbage cans, and make their dens in disused buildings and outhouses.

The fox and other species that thrive in urban environments are exceptional, however. The great majority of animal species

Protection or Mates?

Guppies are small fish that live in streams in central America and the West Indies. The male is considerably smaller than the female and much more brightly colored, being adorned with an array of red, blue, black, and iridescent spots and patches. There is considerable variation from stream to stream in terms of how colorful males are, the most colorful males being found where there are fewer predatory fish. Experimental studies have shown, first, that female guppies prefer to mate with colorful males rather than dull ones; second, that in populations exposed to heavy predation, males become markedly less brightly colored over the course of about 10 generations. For an individual male, therefore, there is a trade-off: if he is very brightly colored he will be attractive to females, but will be conspicuous to predators; if he is dull he is less likely to be eaten but may not attract any mates. This trade-off leads to there being different degrees of male coloration in different streams, depending on the number of predators found there.

△ New environments favor new adaptations, fuelling the process of evolution. A stream with relatively few predators provides an opportunity for male guppies to adopt colors that attract females; male guppies that live in streams with an abundance of predators are less conspicuous.

Female preference is also influenced by local variation in the number of predators. Where predators are numerous, the strength of the female preference for brighter males is less strong than where they are absent. Male guppies also show variation in their behavior in response to short-term changes in their environment. They perform courtship displays less often and less vigorously during the middle part of the day, when the light is bright and they are more conspicuous to predators. They can also detect the presence of predatory fish and become less active in courtship when predators are present.

have not been able to adapt to human impacts on their environment and many have become extinct or are on the verge of becoming so. Unless we humans can alter our behavior, we face a future in which the greatly altered environment that we are creating will support only a tiny fraction of the species that currently inhabit the earth. Many of those that do survive alongside us will be regarded as pests. Foxes, for example, are carriers of rabies, and birds such as gulls can be a serious nuisance in large numbers.

Humans, then, will be the custodians of an impoverished world in which we will be in constant conflict with many of the species that do manage to persist. The fact that those species have the inherent capacity to adapt to changes in their environment will mean that the battle to control them will be a complex and expensive task.

◁ It is tempting to assume that the majority of animals can adapt to human impacts as readily as a hummingbird nesting on a light fixture, but the truth is that our activities have led to the endangerment or extinction of hundreds of animal species; indeed, we regard many animals that manage to survive alongside us as pests.

Notes on Contributors

R. ROBIN BAKER received his B.Sc. and Ph.D. from the University of Bristol, England, where he later became a Science Research Council Postdoctoral Fellow. He is presently a Reader in Zoology at the University of Manchester and is best known for his work on human navigation and magnetoreception, and human sperm competition. He is the author of nine books, including *The Evolutionary Ecology of Animal Migration* 1978, *Bird Navigation — The Solution of a Mystery?* 1984 and *Human Navigation and Magnetoreception* 1989.

PETER BERTHOLD studied for his doctorate at Tubingen University, the subject of his thesis was the reproductive cycle and its control in the starling. He has been Professor of Zoology at Constance University, Germany and was President of the Deutsche Ornithologen Gesellschaft. Since 1970 he has been involved in the 'Mettnau Reir Illmitz Program', a long-term bird trapping and examination program.

DANIELLE CLODE completed a bachelor's degree in Psychology at Adelaide University, South Australia. Upon receiving a Rhodes scholarship she moved to Oxford University where she works with the Wildlife Conservation Research Unit. In the past she has studied the behavioral requirements of fennec foxes in captivity, enabling them to be kept and bred successfully. This interest in carnivores, and aspects of conservation, has led her to work on the effects of introduced predators on native species. She is currently researching the impact of feral mink predation on endangered seabird colonies in the Outer Hebrides of Scotland.

JOSHUA R. GINSBERG was educated in the United States and England. He completed a bachelor's degree in Palaeontology at Yale University and an M.A. and Ph.D. on the behavior and ecology of the Grevy's zebra in northern Kenya at Princeton. For the past five years he has run a research project on the behavior, ecology, and conservation of the African wild dog in Zimbabwe's Hwange National Park. Prior to this, he was a NATO Research Fellow and Wolfson College Junior Research Fellow at Oxford University.

DEBORAH M. GORDON is an Assistant Professor in the Department of Biological Sciences at Stanford University, California. She was previously a Research Associate at the Centre for Population Biology, Imperial College, at Silwood Park, England, a Research Fellow at Lady Margaret Hall, Oxford University, a NATO postdoctoral fellow at the Centre for Mathematical Biology, Oxford and a Junior Fellow at Harvard University, Massachusetts.

MARION HALL completed her bachelor's degree and D.Phil. at Sussex University, England. Since then she has lectured in zoology at the University of Gezira in Sudan and worked in scientific publishing as Assistant Editor of the journal Animal Behaviour. She is now a Course Manager in the Biology Department at the Open University, Milton Keynes and is researching dominance and territoriality in peacocks.

TIM HALLIDAY is a Doctor of Philosophy (Oxon.) and has taught at The Open University since 1977. He is currently Professor in Biology and Head of the Biology Department at The Open University. Professor Halliday is also a member of the Council of the Zoological Society of London and is the chairman of its Conservation and Consultancy Committee.

MICHAEL HANSELL studied for his B.A. in Zoology at Trinity College, Dublin, and his D.Phil. at Oxford University. His doctorate research project was on the case building of caddis larvae and laid the foundations for a lifetime interest in animal building behavior. He has lectured at the University of Khartoum and is presently a Senior Lecturer at the University of Glasgow since 1968.

SUE HEALY was born in New Zealand and gained her bachelor's degree in Zoology and Physiology before completing a D.Phil. in Zoology at St Hilda's Collage, Oxford University. She is at present a Junior Research Fellow at St John's College, Oxford University and will shortly take up a lectureship in Psychology at the University of Newcastle. Her research interests center around animal learning and memory, in particular spatial memory and the relationship between behavior and parts of the brain, specifically the relationship between food storing and the hippocampus.

CHARLOTTE A. HOSIE studied Biological Sciences at Leicester University, England. Her Ph.D. was carried out at the Open University, Milton Keynes, on the subject of the sexual motivation of female newts. She is presently a Research Fellow at the Open University, studying the intricacies of newt courtship behavior.

FELICITY HUNTINGFORD studied for her B.A. in Zoology and Ph.D. in Psychology at Oxford University. She is currently a Reader in Zoology at Glasgow University. Her research interests include the behavior of freshwater fish, including their aggressive interactions and is currently engaged in a series of studies of aggression in salmonid fish and how this relates to food acquisition, growth and life history patterns.

RAYMOND B. HUEY is currently Professor of Zoology at the University of Washington, Seattle. He received his B.A. in Zoology from the University of California, his M.A. in Zoology from the University of Texas and his Ph.D. in Biology from Harvard University. His main research is on evolution of physiology in lizards and in fruit flies, senescence in natural populations, and the thermal biology of ectotherms. He has done extensive field work in North and South America, the Caribbean, Australia, and Africa.

TERENCE LINDSEY was born in England, raised and educated in Canada and has made Australia his home for the past 20 years. He is an Associate of the Australian Museum and a part-time tutor at the University of Sydney. His special area of interest is the reproduction and foraging strategies of birds.

DAVID J. ROBINSON is a Lecturer in Biology at the Open University, Milton Keynes and he has worked there since 1981, when he moved from Edinburgh University, Scotland. His particular interest is in animal sound and has recently acted as a consultant on sound for the multimedia Encyclopedia of Mammalian Biology on Compact Disc.

ANGELA K. TURNER is currently Managing Editor of the journal Animal Behaviour and is the author of *Swallows and Martins of the World* (1989), and *Animal Conflict* with Felicity Huntingford (1987). Her particular area of interest is in aerial feeding birds. She studied swallows and sand martins in Scotland for her Ph.D. and later blue-and-white swallows in Venezuela and swiftlets in Malaysia.

INDEX

ACKNOWLEDGMENTS

Picture Credits

Heather Angel: page 22 bottom.

Anglo-Australian Observatory: page 130 top (David Malin).

Aquila Photographics: page 21 (C. & T. Stuart); page 59 top (Wayne Lankinen).

Ardea London: page 15 top (John Clegg); page 18 (Hans & Judy Beste); page 19 (P. Morris); page 60 top right (Stefan Meyers); page 68 top; pages 75 top and 121 bottom (Alan Weaving); page 87 bottom (John Mason); page 126 bottom (Eric Dragesco).

Auscape International: pages 8 left, 33 bottom, 35 top left, 37 bottom, 84 bottom, 97, 102 and 120 top (Jean-Paul Ferrero); page 8 bottom Jacana (Gunter Ziesler); pages 16, 75 bottom and 86 (Hans & Judy Beste); page 27 bottom Jacana (K. Ross); page 31 (Roger Brown); page 32 Jacana (Martial Colas); page 36 (Jack & Lindsay Cupper); pages 38, 96 and 120 bottom (Ferrero/Labat); page 44 bottom (Anup & Manoj Shah); pages 47 top and 93 bottom (Graham Robertson); pages 47 bottom and 116 bottom (Tui De Roy); page 48 top and bottom (John Shaw); page 49 top (Colin Monteath); page 51 top (M. W. Gillam); page 54 bottom (Esther Beaton); page 80 Jacana (Alain Degre); page 87 top (Merlin Tuttle); pages 88 and 128 (D. Parer & E. Parer-Cook); page 105 (Sophie De Wilde); page 136 (Mark Jones); page 138 top (Jean-Michel Labat).

Austral International: contents top right Sipa-Press; pages 10/11 and 109 Camera Press (Hans Pfletschinger); page 71 bottom Sygma (Remi Amann); page 133 Rex Features.

Australian Picture Library: page 9 top Zefa-Allstock, page 112.

Densey Clyne: page 67 top.

Australasian Nature Transparencies: 72 bottom (Otto Rogge)

Bruce Coleman Ltd.: pages 14 and 95 bottom right (Alain Compost); page 22 top (George McCarthy); page 24 top (Jan Van De Kam); page 34 top (John Cancalosi); pages 35 top right and 71 top left (Konrad Wothe); page 35 bottom (Ferrero/Labat); page 46 (Charlie Ott); page 51 bottom right (Kim Taylor); page 58 top (Gunter Ziesler); page 59 bottom (Roger Coggan); page 61 top (S. Nielsen); pages 61 bottom, 76 top right, 85 bottom, 91 bottom, 93 top and 106 (Jane Burton); pages 62 bottom, 90, 95 bottom left and 129 top (Jeff Foott); page 71 center right (Gary Retherford); page 74 (John Visser); page 75 center (M. P. L. Fogden); pages 83 bottom, 91 top and 126 top (Hans Reinhard); page 99 (Erwin & Peggy Bauer); page 103 (Jan Van De Kam); page 107 bottom (W. S. Paton); page 108 top (Michael Freeman); pages 113 and 119 top (John Shaw); page 114 top (John Cancalosi); page 115 (Austin James Steven); page 116 top (Jen & Des Bartlett); page 124 top left (Peter Davey); page 134 top (E. Duscher); page 135 (Adrian Davies); page 137 (Leonard Lee Rue III).

Michael & Patricia Fogden: pages 9 bottom, 20 and 81.

Frank Lane Picture Agency: pages 15 bottom and 50 bottom (Silvestris); pages 24 bottom and 26 (Mike Rose); page 25 top (L. Lee Rue); page 33 top (Terry Whittaker); pages 54 top and 56 (Eric & David Hosking); page 55 top (Fritz Polking); page 66 (A. R. Hamblin); page 68 bottom (Frank W. Lane); page 83 top left and top right (G. E. Hyde); page 114 bottom (Eichhorn/Zingel); page 119 bottom (Rudolf Hofels); page 131 (W. Wisniewski).

Horizon: title page, contents page bottom right (Tom McHugh); opposite contents page (Stan Wayman); contents page top left (Dr M. P. Kahl); contents page bottom left (Mark N. Boulton); page 12 (Toni Amgermayer); page 13 (Tim Davis); page 37 top; page 40/41 (Mike Lugue); page 64 (James Fisher); page 65 (Harry Angels); page 73 (Paul Zborowski); page 76 bottom left (Darwin Dale); page 77 bottom left (Heidi Ecker).

The Image Bank: page 42 (Guido Alberto Rossi); page 50 top (Cesar Lucas); page 53 bottom right (J. Carmichael Jr); page 55 bottom; page 107 top (Peter Hendrie); pages 123 and 127 (Joe Van Os); page 139 bottom (Franklin Wagner).

International Photo Library: endpapers and opposite imprint page.

Leo Meier: page 17 top and bottom.

Natural Science Photos: page 118 top (Martin Harvey); page 124 top right (Curtis E.Williams); page 134 bottom (Richard Revels).

NHPA: page 28 (Hellio & Van Ingen); pages 52 and 67 bottom (George Bernard); page 77 bottom right (J. Jeffrey); page 84 top (Dr Ivan Polunin); page 92 (Manfred Danegger); page 118 bottom (Robert Erwin).

Oxford Scientific Films: Back cover and page 89 (Konrad Wothe); page 25 bottom (D. H. Thompson); page 27 top (Tui De Roy); page 30 top (Ben Osborne); page 34 bottom (Steve Turner); page 39 (David Cayless); pages 51 bottom left and 62 top (Tom Ulrich); page 57 (Gordon Maclean); page 69 (Eyal Bartov); page 70 (J. A. L. Cooke); page 78/79 (Doug Allan); page 94 top (Martyn Colbeck); page 104 (Michele Hall); page 110/111 (Wendy Shattil & Bob Rozinski); page 117 top (C. M. Perrins); page 125 (Owen Newman) page 138 bottom (Rodger Jackman); page 139 top left and top right (Max Gibbs).

The Photo Library — Sydney: cover (Kenneth Fink); page 9 right Photo Researchers Inc., 53 bottom left and page 132.

Planet Earth Pictures: page 29 (K. A. Puttock); page 43 (David P. Maitland); page 44 top (Matthews & Purdy); pages 45 bottom, 60 top left, 108 bottom, 122 and 129 bottom (Jonathan Scott); page 72 top (Peter Scoones); page 82 (Doug Perrine); page 117 bottom (Georgette Douwma); page 121 top (Hans Christian Heap).

Survival Anglia: page 30 bottom (Joel Bennett); pages 45 top, 58 bottom and 94 bottom (Jeff Foott); page 58 bottom (David Shale).